Ancient Texts and the Bible
Book 2 - Easy Reader Edition

In The Beginning...
From Noah to Abraham

Minister 2 Others

Ancient Texts and the Bible
Book 2

In The Beginning... From Noah to Abraham

Easy Reader Edition

In The Beginning... From Noah to Abraham
ISBN 978-1-947751-20-0

Ancient texts compiled for this series:

The Bible
King James Version 1769

The Book of Enoch
An English translation by Dr. Laurence,
Archbishop of Cashel,
Formerly professor of Hebrew at Oxford, 1833

The Book of Jasher
Faithfully translated 1840
From the original Hebrew into English
Published by J.H. Parry & Company 1887

The Book of Jubilees
By R.H. Charles, Oxford: Clarendon Press, 1913

Ancient Texts and the Bible

series include:

Book 1: In The Beginning... From Adam to Noah

Book 2: In The Beginning... From Noah to Abraham

Book 3: In The Beginning... From Abraham to Israel

Book 4: In The Beginning... From Israel to Egypt

Book 5: In The Beginning... From Egypt to Goshen

Book 6: Israel... From Goshen to Sinai

Book 7: Israel... From Sinai to the Tabernacle

Book 8: Israel... Through the Book of Leviticus

Book 9: Israel... Through the Book of Numbers

Book 10: Israel... Through the Book of Joshua

Table of Contents:

Forward

The **Ancient Texts and the Bible** series synchronizes the manuscripts of Enoch, Jasher, and Jubilees into the Bible, making one complete storyline. The books are interwoven using the Torah as the backbone, and the extra-biblical texts as the fleshing out of that backbone.

The second book in this series contains Genesis chapters 6 - 17, as well as parts in the following books: Enoch chapters 1 - 21, 53 - 57, 63 - 68, 79; Jasher chapters 4-17; and Jubilees chapters 5-15.

Though the language in the writings have been updated, replacing words like "*thou*" and "*thine*" with words like "*you*" and "*your*", the integrity of the verses remain.

The "*Easy Reader*" edition is for those who just want to read the storyline and enjoy the journey. The stop signs and complex formatting have been removed so one may merely focus upon the story being told.

The *Expanded Edition* of **Ancient Texts and the Bible** was created for the more studious reader. The various manuscripts have the following formatting applied to them in this edition:

the Bible - Regular

THE BOOK OF ENOCH - ALL CAPITALS

the Book of Jasher - Italics

<u>the Book of Jubilees - Underlined</u>

Where one of the extra-biblical texts reiterates the Bible, the phrase is then put in a **bold font**. Where two manuscripts overlap each other exclusive of the Bible, then both fonts are used. For instance, where Jasher and Jubilees intercept, the text is then formatted as *Italics and Underlined.*

The stop sign is another element to the *Expanded Edition* that is not seen in the *Easy Reader*. This image points to contradictions in the content. Printed versions also contain page numbers within the stop sign revealing the page where contradictory information is located, and vice versa. This information was not feasible to place in the e-book versions since the page numbers vary depending on the font size the reader chooses. Following, is an example from each edition:

Easy Reader Edition:

> (Genesis 6:1) (Enoch 7:1) (Jubilees 5:1...)
> And it came to pass, when the children of men began to multiply on the face of the earth, and daughters were born to them, elegant and beautiful.

Expanded Edition:

> (Genesis 6:1) (ENOCH 7:1) (Jubilees 5:1...)
> **And it came to pass, when** THE CHILDREN OF **men began to multiply on the face of the earth**, **and daughters were born to them**, ELEGANT AND BEAUTIFUL.

Whichever you choose, may you ***Enjoy the Journey***!

Prologue

(Enoch 1:1)
The word of the blessing of Enoch, how he blessed the elect and the righteous, who were to exist in the time of trouble; rejecting all the wicked and ungodly. Enoch, a righteous man, who was with God, answered and spoke, while his eyes were open, and while he saw a holy vision in the heavens. This the angels showed me.

(Enoch 1:2)
From them I heard all things, and understood what I saw; that which will not take place in this generation, but in a generation which is to succeed at a distant period, on account of the elect.

(Enoch 1:3)
Upon their account, I spoke and conversed with him, who will go forth from his habitation, the Holy and Mighty One, the God of the world:

(Enoch 1:4)
Who will hereafter tread upon Mount Sinai; appear with his hosts; and be manifested in the strength of his power from heaven.

(Enoch 1:5)
All shall be afraid, and the Watchers be terrified.

(Enoch 1:6)
Great fear and trembling shall seize them, even to the ends

of the earth. The lofty mountains shall be troubled, and the exalted hills depressed, melting like a honeycomb in the flame. The earth shall be immerged, and all things which are in it perish; while judgment shall come upon all, even upon all the righteous:

(Enoch 1:8)
But to them shall he give peace: he shall preserve the elect, and exercise clemency towards them.

(Enoch 1:9)
Then shall all belong to God; be happy and blessed; and the splendor of the Godhead shall illuminate them.

~ ~ ~

(Enoch 20:1)
These are the names of the angels who watch.

(Enoch 20:2)
Uriel, one of the holy angels, who presides over clamor and terror.

(Enoch 20:3)
Raphael, one of the holy angels, who presides over the spirits of men.

(Enoch 20:4)
Raguel, one of the holy angels, who inflicts punishment on the world and the luminaries.

(Enoch 20:5)
Michael, one of the holy angels, who, presiding over human virtue, commands the nations.

(Enoch 20:6)
Sarakiel, one of the holy angels, who presides over the spirits of the children of men that transgress.

(Enoch 20:7)
Gabriel, one of the holy angels, who presides over Ikisat, over paradise, and over the cherubim.

~ ~ ~

(Enoch 21:1)
Then I made a circuit to a place in which nothing was completed.

(Enoch 21:2)
And there I beheld neither the tremendous workmanship of an exalted heaven, nor of an established earth, but a desolate spot, prepared, and terrific.

(Enoch 21:3)
There, too, I beheld seven stars of heaven bound in it together, like great mountains, and like a blazing fire. I exclaimed, for what species of crime have they been bound, and why have they been removed to this place? Then Uriel, one of the holy angels who was with me, and who conducted me, answered: Enoch, why do you ask; why reason with yourself, and anxiously inquire? These are those of the stars which have

transgressed the commandment of the Most High God; and are here bound, until the infinite number of the days of their crimes be completed.

(Enoch 21:4)
From there I afterwards passed on to another terrific place;

(Enoch 21:5)
Where I beheld the operation of a great fire blazing and glittering, in the midst of which there was a division. Columns of fire struggled together to the end of the abyss, and deep was their descent. But neither its measurement nor magnitude was I able to discover; neither could I perceive its origin. Then I exclaimed, how terrible is this place, and how difficult to explore!

(Enoch 21:6)
Uriel, one of the holy angels who was with me, answered and said: Enoch, why are you alarmed and amazed at this terrific place, at the sight of this place of suffering? This, he said, Is the prison of the angels; and here they are kept forever.

Genesis: Chapter Six

(Genesis 6:1) (Enoch 7:1) (Jubilees 5:1...)
And it came to pass, when the children of men began to multiply on the face of the earth, and daughters were born to them, elegant and beautiful.

(Genesis 6:2) (Enoch 7:2) (...Jubilees 5:1...)
That the sons of God, the sons of heaven, saw the daughters of men on a certain year of this jubilee, that they were beautiful to look on; they became enamored of them saying to each other, Come, let us select for ourselves wives from the progeny of men, and let us beget children.

(Enoch 7:3)
Then their leader Samyaza said to them; I fear that you may perhaps be indisposed to the performance of this enterprise;

(Enoch 7:4)
And that I alone shall suffer for so grievous a crime.

(Enoch 7:5)
But they answered him and said; We all swear;

(Enoch 7:6)
And bind ourselves by mutual execrations, that we will not change our intention, but execute our projected undertaking.

(Enoch 7:7)
Then they swore all together, and all bound themselves by

mutual execrations. Their whole number was two hundred, who descended on Ardis, which is the top of Mount Armon.

(Enoch 7:8)
That mountain therefore was called Armon, because they had sworn on it, and bound themselves by mutual execrations.

(Enoch 7:9)
These are the names of their chiefs: Samyaza, who was their leader, Urakabarameel, Akibeel, Tamiel, Ramuel, Danel, Azkeel, Saraknyal, Asael, Armers, Batraal, Anane, Zavebe, Samsaveel, Ertael, Turel, Yomyael, Arazyal. These were the prefects of the two hundred angels, and the remainder were all with them.

(Genesis 6:2) (Enoch 7:10) (...Jubilees 5:1...)
And they took them wives of all which they chose, each choosing for himself; whom they began to approach, and with whom they cohabited; teaching them sorcery, incantations, and the dividing of roots and trees.

(Enoch 7:11) (...jubilees 5:1)
And the women conceiving bore to them sons and they were giants.

(Enoch 7:12)
Whose stature was each three hundred cubits. These devoured all which the labor of men produced; until it became impossible to feed them;

(Enoch 7:13)
When they turned themselves against men, in order to devour them;

(Enoch 7:14)
And began to injure birds, beasts, reptiles, and fishes, to eat their flesh one after another, and to drink their blood.

(Enoch 7:15)
Then the earth reproved the unrighteous.

~ ~ ~

(Enoch 8:1)
Moreover, Azazyel taught men to make swords, knives, shields, breastplates, the fabrication of mirrors, and the workmanship of bracelets and ornaments, the use of paint, the beautifying of the eyebrows, the use of stones of every valuable and select kind, and of all sorts of dyes, so that the world became altered.

(Enoch 8:2)
Impiety increased; fornication multiplied; and they transgressed and corrupted all their ways.

(Enoch 8:3)
Amazarak taught all the sorcerers, and dividers of roots:

(Enoch 8:4)
Armers taught the solution of sorcery;

(Enoch 8:5)
Barkayal taught the observers of the stars;

(Enoch 8:6)
Akibeel taught signs;

(Enoch 8:7)
Tamiel taught astronomy;

(Enoch 8:8)
And Asaradel taught the motion of the moon.

(Enoch 8:9)
And men, being destroyed, cried out; and their voice reached to heaven.

~ ~ ~

(Enoch 63)
I saw also other countenances in that secret place. I heard the voice of an angel, saying, These are the angels who have descended from heaven to earth, and have revealed secrets to the sons of men, and have seduced the sons of men to the commission of sin.

~ ~ ~

(Jasher 4:16)
And all the sons of men departed from the ways of the Lord in those days as they multiplied on the face of the earth with sons and daughters, and they taught one another their evil practices and they continued sinning against the Lord.

(Jasher 4:17)
And every man made to himself a God, and they robbed and plundered every man his neighbor as well as his relative, and they corrupted the earth, and the earth was filled with violence.

(Jasher 4:18)
And their judges and rulers went to the daughters of men and took their wives by force from their husbands according to their choice, and the sons of men in those days took from the cattle of the earth, the beasts of the field and the birds of the air, and taught the mixture of animals of one species with the other, in order therewith to provoke the Lord; and God saw the whole earth and it was corrupt, for all flesh had corrupted its ways on earth, all men and all animals.

(Genesis 6:3) (Jubilees 5:8)
And the Lord said, My spirit shall not always strive with man, for that he also is flesh: yet his days shall be a hundred and twenty years.

(Enoch 79: 3)
In the days of sinners, the years shall be shortened.

(Enoch 79:4)
Their seed shall be backward in their prolific soil; and everything done on earth shall be subverted, and disappear in its season. The rain shall be restrained, and heaven shall stand still.

(Enoch 79:5)
In those days, the fruits of the earth shall be late, and not flourish in their season; and in their season the fruits of the trees shall be withhold.

(Enoch 79:6)
The moon shall change its laws, and not be seen at its proper period. But in those days, shall heaven be seen; and barrenness shall take place in the borders of the great chariots in the west. Heaven shall shine more than when illuminated by the orders of light; while many chiefs among the stars of authority shall err, perverting their ways and works.

(Enoch 79:7)
Those shall not appear in their season, who command them, and all the classes of the stars shall be shut up against sinners.

(Enoch 79:8)
The thoughts of those who dwell on earth shall transgress within them; and they shall be perverted in all their ways.

(Enoch 79:9)
They shall transgress, and think themselves gods; while evil shall be multiplied among them.

(Enoch 79:10)
And punishment shall come on them, so that all of them shall be destroyed.

(Genesis 6:4)

There were giants in the earth in those days; and also after that, when the sons of God came in to the daughters of men, and they bore children to them, the same became mighty men which were of old, men of renown.

(Genesis 6:5) (Jubilees 5:2)

And lawlessness increased on the earth and all flesh corrupted its way, alike men and cattle and beasts and birds and everything that walks on the earth - all of them corrupted their ways and their orders, and they began to devour each other, and lawlessness increased on the earth. And God saw that the wickedness of man was great in the earth, and that every imagination of the thoughts of his heart, of all men, was only evil continually.

(Jubilees 5:3)
And God looked on the earth, and behold it was corrupt, and all flesh had corrupted its orders, and all that were on the earth had wrought all manner of evil before His eyes.

~ ~ ~

(Enoch 9:1)
Then Michael and Gabriel, Raphael, Suryal, and Uriel, looked down from heaven, and saw the quantity of blood which was shed on earth, and all the iniquity which was done on it, and said one to another, it is the voice of their cries;

(Enoch 9:2)
The earth deprived of her children has cried even to the gate of heaven.

(Enoch 9:3)
And now to you, O you holy ones of heaven, the souls of men complain, saying, Obtain justice for us with the Most High. Then they said to their Lord, the king, you are Lord of lords, God of gods, king of kings. The throne of your glory is forever and ever, and forever and ever is your name sanctified and glorified. You are blessed and glorified.

(Enoch 9:4)
You have made all things; you possess power over all things; and all things are open and manifest before you. You behold all things, and nothing, can be concealed from you.

(Enoch 9:5)
You have seen what Azazyel has done, how he as taught every species of iniquity on earth, and has disclosed to the world all the secret things which are done in the heavens.

(Enoch 9:6)
Samyaza also has taught sorcery, to whom you have given authority over those who are associated with him. They have gone together to the daughters of men; have lain with them; have become polluted;

(Enoch 9:7)
And have discovered crimes to them.

(Enoch 9:8)
The women likewise have brought forth giants.

(Enoch 9:9)
Thus, has the whole earth been filled with blood and with iniquity.

(Enoch 9:10)
And now, behold, the souls of those who are dead, cry out.

(Enoch 9:11)
And complain even to the gate of heaven.

(Enoch 9:12)
Their groaning ascends; nor can they escape from the

unrighteousness which is committed on earth. You know all things, before they exist.

(Enoch 9:13)
You know these things, and what has been done by them; yet you do not speak to us.

(Enoch 9:14)
What ought we to do to them on account of these things?

~ ~ ~

(Enoch 10:1)
Then the Most High, the Great and Holy One spoke,

(Enoch 10:2)
And sent Arsayalalyur to the son of Lamech,

(Enoch 10:3)
Saying, Say to him in my name, Conceal yourself.

(Enoch 10:4)
Then explain to him the consummation which is about to take place; for all the earth shall perish; the waters of a deluge shall come over the whole earth, and all things which are in it shall be destroyed.

(Enoch 10:5)
And now teach him how he may escape, and how his seed may remain in all the earth.

(Enoch 10:6)
Again, the Lord said to Raphael, Bind Azazyel hand and foot; cast him into darkness; and opening the desert which is in Dudael, cast him in there.

(Enoch 10:7)
Throw on him hurled and pointed stones, covering him with darkness;

(Enoch 10:8)
There shall he remain forever; cover his face, that he may not see the light.

(Enoch 10:9)
And in the great day of judgment let him be cast into the fire.

(Enoch 10:10)
Restore the earth, which the angels have corrupted; and announce life to it, that I may revive it.

(Enoch 10:11)
All the sons of men shall not perish in consequence of every secret, by which the Watchers have destroyed, and which they have taught, their offspring.

(Enoch 10:12)
All the earth has been corrupted by the effects of the teaching of Azazyel. To him therefore ascribe the whole crime.

(Jubilees 5:6)
And against the angels whom He had sent on the earth, He was exceedingly wroth, and He gave commandment to root them out of all their dominion, and He bade us to bind them

in the depths of the earth, and behold they are bound in the midst of them, and are kept separate.

(Jubilees 5:7)
And against their sons went forth a command from before His face that they should be smitten with the sword, and be removed from under heaven.

(Enoch 10:13)
To Gabriel also the Lord said, Go to the biters, to the reprobates, to the children of fornication; and destroy the children of fornication, the offspring of the Watchers, from among men; bring them forth, and excite them one against another. Let them perish by mutual slaughter; for length of days shall not be theirs.

(Enoch 10:14)
They shall all entreat you, but their fathers shall not obtain their wishes respecting them; for they shall hope for eternal life, and that they may live, each of them, five hundred years.

(Jubilees 5:9)
And He sent His sword into their midst that each should slay his neighbor, and they began to slay each other till they all fell by the sword and were destroyed from the earth.

(Jubilees 5:10)
And their fathers were witnesses, and after this they were bound in the depths of the earth forever, until the day of the great condemnation, when judgment is executed on all those who have corrupted their ways and their works before the Lord.

(Jubilees 5:11)
And He destroyed all from their places, and there was not left one of them whom He judged not according to all their wickedness.

(Jubilees 5:12)
And he made for all his works a new and righteous nature, so that they should not sin in their whole nature forever, but should be all righteous each in his kind always.

(Jubilees 5:13)
And the judgment of all is ordained and written on the heavenly tablets in righteousness - even all who depart from the path which is ordained for them to walk in; and if they walk not therein, judgment is written down for every creature and for every kind.

(Jubilees 5:14)
And there is nothing in heaven or on earth, or in light or in darkness, or in Sheol or in the depth, or in the place of darkness which is not judged; and all their judgments are ordained and written and engraved.

(Jubilees 5:15)
In regard to all He will judge, the great according to his greatness, and the small according to his smallness, and each according to his way.

(Jubilees 5:16)
And He is not one who will regard the person, nor is He one who will receive gifts, if He says that He will execute judgment on each: if one gave everything that is on the earth, He will not regard the gifts or the person, nor accept anything at his hands, for He is a righteous judge.

(Jubilees 5:17)
And of the children of Israel it has been written and ordained: If they turn to him in righteousness He will forgive all their transgressions and pardon all their sins.

(Jubilees 5:18)
It is written and ordained that He will show mercy to all who turn from all their guilt once each year.

(Enoch 10:15)
To Michael likewise the Lord said, Go and announce his crime to Samyaza, and to the others who are with him, who have been associated with women, that they might be polluted with all their impurity. And when all their sons shall be slain, when they shall see the perdition of their beloved, bind them for seventy generations underneath the earth, even to the day of judgment, and of consummation, until the judgment, the effect of which will last forever, be completed.

(Enoch 10:16)
Then shall they be taken away into the lowest depths of the fire in torments; and in confinement shall they be shut up forever.

(Enoch 10:17)
Immediately after this shall he, together with them, burn and perish; they shall be bound until the consummation of many generations.

(Enoch 10:18)
Destroy all the souls addicted to dalliance, and the offspring of the Watchers, for they have tyrannized over mankind.

(Enoch 10:19)
Let every oppressor perish from the face of the earth;

(Enoch 10:20)
Let every evil work be destroyed;

(Enoch 10:21)
The plant of righteousness and of rectitude appear, and its produce become a blessing.

(Enoch 10:22)
Righteousness and rectitude shall be forever planted with delight.

(Enoch 10:23)
And then shall all the saints give thanks, and live until they have begotten a thousand children, while the whole period of their youth, and their sabbaths shall be completed in peace. In those days, all the earth shall be cultivated in righteousness; it shall be wholly planted with trees, and filled with benediction; every tree of delight shall be planted in it.

(Enoch 10:24)
In it shall vines be planted; and the vine which shall be planted in it shall yield fruit to satiety; every seed, which shall be sown in it, shall produce for one measure a thousand; and one measure of olives shall produce ten presses of oil.

(Enoch 10:25)
Purify the earth from all oppression, from all injustice, from all crime, from all impiety, and from all the pollution which is committed on it. Exterminate them from the earth.

(Enoch 10:26)
Then shall all the children of men be righteous, and all nations shall pay me divine honors, and bless me; and all shall adore me.

(Enoch 10:27)
The earth shall be cleansed from all corruption, from every crime, from all punishment, and from all suffering; neither will I again send a deluge on it from generation to generation forever.

~ ~ ~

(Enoch 11:1)
In those days, I will open the treasures of blessing which are in heaven, that I may cause them to descend on earth, and on all the works and labor of man.

(Enoch 11:2)
Peace and equity shall associate with the sons of men all the days of the world, in every generation of it.

~ ~ ~

(Enoch 12:1)
Before all these things Enoch was concealed; nor did any one of the sons of men know where he was concealed, where he had been, and what had happened.

(Enoch 12:2)
He was wholly engaged with the holy ones, and with the Watchers in his days.

(Enoch 12:3)
I, Enoch, was blessing the great Lord and king of peace.

(Enoch 12:4)
And behold the Watchers called me Enoch the scribe.

(Enoch 12:5)
Then the Lord said to me: Enoch, scribe of righteousness, go tell the Watchers of heaven, who have deserted the lofty sky, and their holy everlasting station, who have been polluted with women.

(Enoch 12:6)
And have done as the sons of men do, by taking to themselves wives, and who have been greatly corrupted on the earth;

(Enoch 12:7)
That on the earth they shall never obtain peace and remission of sin. For they shall not rejoice in their offspring; they shall behold the slaughter of their beloved; shall lament for the destruction of their sons; and shall petition forever; but shall not obtain mercy and peace.

~ ~ ~

(Enoch 13:1)
Then Enoch, passing on, said to Azazyel: you shall not obtain

peace. A great sentence is gone forth against you. He shall bind you;

(Enoch 13:2)
Neither shall relief, mercy, and supplication be your, on account of the oppression which you have taught;

(Enoch 13:3)
And on account of every act of blasphemy, tyranny, and sin, which you have discovered to the children of men.

(Enoch 13:4)
Then departing from him I spoke to them all together;

(Enoch 13:5)
And they all became terrified, and trembled;

(Enoch 13:6)
Beseeching me to write for them a memorial of supplication, that they might obtain forgiveness; and that I might make the memorial of their prayer ascend up before the God of heaven; because they could not themselves from there on out address him, nor raise up their eyes to heaven on account of the disgraceful offence for which they were judged.

(Enoch 13:7)
Then I wrote a memorial of their prayer and supplication, for their spirits, for everything which they was done, and for the subject of their entreaty, that they might obtain remission and rest.

(Enoch 13:8)
Proceeding on, I continued over the waters of Danbadan, which is on the right to the west of Armon, reading the

memorial of their prayer, until I fell asleep.

(Enoch 13:9)
And behold a dream came to me, and visions appeared above me. I fell down and saw a vision of punishment, that I might relate it to the sons of heaven, and reprove them. When I awoke I went to them. All being collected together stood weeping in Oubelseyael, which is situated between Libanos and Seneser, with their faces veiled.

(Enoch 13:10)
I related in their presence all the visions which I had seen, and my dream;

(Enoch 13:11)
And began to utter these words of righteousness, reproving the Watchers of heaven.

~ ~ ~

(Enoch 14:1)
This is the book of the words of righteousness, and of the reproof of the Watchers, who belong to the world, according to that which he, who is holy and great, commanded in the vision. I perceived in my dream, that I was now speaking with a tongue of flesh, and with my breath, which the Mighty One has put into the mouth of men, that they might converse with it.

(Enoch 14:2)
And understand with the heart. As he has created and given to

men the power of comprehending the word of understanding, so has he created and given to me the power of reproving the Watchers, the offspring of heaven. I have written your petition; and in my vision it has been shown me, that what you request will not be granted you as long as the world endures.

(Enoch 14:3)
Judgment has been passed on you: your request will not be granted you.

(Enoch 14:4)
From this time forward, never shall you ascend into heaven; he has said that on the earth he will bind you, as long as the world endures.

(Enoch 14:5)
But before these things you shall behold the destruction of your beloved sons; you shall not possess them, but they shall fall before you by the sword.

(Enoch 14:6)
Neither shall you entreat for them, nor for yourselves;

(Enoch 14:7)
But you shall weep and supplicate in silence. The words of the book which I wrote.

(Enoch 14:8)
A vision thus appeared to me.

(Enoch 14:9)
Behold, in that vision clouds and a mist invited me; agitated stars and flashes of lightning impelled and pressed me

forwards, while winds in the vision assisted my flight, accelerating my progress.

(Enoch 14:10)
They elevated me aloft to heaven. I proceeded, until I arrived at a wall built with stones of crystal. A vibrating flame surrounded it, which began to strike me with terror.

(Enoch 14:11)
Into this vibrating flame I entered;

(Enoch 14:12)
And drew nigh to a spacious habitation built also with stones of crystal. Its walls too, as well as pavement, were formed with stones of crystal, and crystal likewise was the ground. Its roof had the appearance of agitated stars and flashes of lightning; and among them were cherubim of fire in a stormy sky. A flame burned around its walls; and its portal blazed with fire. When I entered into this dwelling, it was hot as fire and cold as ice. No trace of delight or of life was there. Terror overwhelmed me, and a fearful shaking seized me.

(Enoch 14:13)
Violently agitated and trembling, I fell on my face. In the vision I looked,

(Enoch 14:14)
And behold, there was another habitation more spacious than the former, every entrance to which was open before me, erected in the midst of a vibrating flame.

(Enoch 14:15)
So greatly it excelled in all points, in glory, in magnificence, and in magnitude, that it is impossible to describe to you

either the splendor or the extent of it.

(Enoch 14:16)
Its floor was on fire; above were lightnings and agitated stars, while its roof exhibited a blazing fire.

(Enoch 14:17)
Attentively I surveyed it, and saw that it contained an exalted throne;

(Enoch 14:18)
The appearance of which was like that of frost; while its circumference resembled the orb of the brilliant sun; and there was the voice of the cherubim.

(Enoch 14:19)
From underneath this mighty throne rivers of flaming fire issued.

(Enoch 14:20)
To look on it was impossible.

(Enoch 14:21)
One great in glory sat on it:

(Enoch 14:22)
Whose robe was brighter than the sun, and whiter than snow.

(Enoch 14:23)
No angel was capable of penetrating to view the face of him, the Glorious and the Effulgent; nor could any mortal behold him. A fire was flaming around him.

(Enoch 14:24)
A fire also of great extent continued to rise up before him; so that not one of those who surrounded him was capable of approaching him, among the myriads of myriads who were before him. To him holy consultation was needless. Yet did not the sanctified, who were near him, depart far from him either by night or by day; nor were they removed from him. I also was so far advanced, with a veil on my face, and trembling. Then the Lord with his own mouth called me, saying, Approach here, Enoch, at my holy word.

(Enoch 14:25)
And he raised me up, making me draw near even to the entrance. My eye was directed to the ground.

~ ~ ~

(Enoch 15:1)
Then addressing me, he spoke and said, Hear, neither be afraid, O righteous Enoch, you scribe of righteousness: approach here, and hear my voice. Go, say to the Watchers of heaven, who have sent you to pray for them, you ought to pray for men, and not men for you.

(Enoch 15:2)
Why have you forsaken the lofty and holy heaven, which endures forever, and have lain with women; have defiled yourselves with the daughters of men; have taken to yourselves wives; have acted like the sons of the earth, and have begotten an impious offspring?

(Enoch 15:3)
You are spiritual, holy, and possessing a life which is eternal, have polluted yourselves with women; have begotten in carnal blood; have lusted in the blood of men; and have done as those who are flesh and blood do.

(Enoch 15:4)
These however die and perish.

(Enoch 15:5)
Therefore, have I given to them wives, that they might cohabit with them; that sons might be born of them; and that this might be transacted upon earth.

(Enoch 15:6)
But you from the beginning were made spiritual, possessing a life which is eternal, and not subject to death forever.

(Enoch 15:7)
Therefore, I did not make wives for you, because, being spiritual, your dwelling is in heaven.

(Enoch 15:8)
Now the giants, who have been born of spirit and of flesh, shall be called upon earth evil spirits, and on earth shall be their habitation. Evil spirits shall proceed from their flesh, because they were created from above; from the holy Watchers was their beginning and primary foundation. Evil spirits shall they be upon earth, and the spirits of the wicked shall they be called. The habitation of the spirits of heaven shall be in heaven; but upon earth shall be the habitation of terrestrial spirits, who are born on earth.

(Enoch 15:9)
The spirits of the giants shall be like clouds, which shall oppress, corrupt, fall, contend, and bruise upon earth.

(Enoch 15:10)
They shall cause lamentation. No food shall they eat; and they shall be thirsty; they shall be concealed, and shall not rise up against the sons of men, and against women; for they come forth during the days of slaughter and destruction.

~ ~ ~

(Enoch 16:1)
And as to the death of the giants, wheresoever their spirits depart from their bodies, let their flesh, that which is perishable, be without judgment. Thus, they shall perish, until the day of the great consummation of the great world. A destruction shall take place of the Watchers and the impious.

(Enoch 16:2)
And now to the Watchers, who have sent you to pray for them, who in the beginning were in heaven,

(Enoch 16:3)
Say, in heaven have you been; secret things, however, have not been manifested to you; yet have you known a reprobated mystery.

(Enoch 16:4)
And this you have related to women in the hardness of your heart, and by that mystery have women and mankind multiplied evils upon the earth.

(Enoch 16:5)
Say to them, you shall never, therefore, obtain peace.

~ ~ ~

(Enoch 17:1)
They raised me up into a certain place, where there was the appearance of a burning fire; and when they pleased they assumed the likeness of men.

(Enoch 17:2)
They carried me to a lofty spot, to a mountain, the top of which reached to heaven.

(Enoch 17:3)
And I beheld the receptacles of light and of thunder at the extremities of the place, where it was deepest. There was a bow of fire, and arrows in their quiver, a sword of fire, and every species of lightning.

(Enoch 17:4)
Then they elevated me to a babbling stream, and to a fire in the west, which received all the setting of the sun. I came to a river of fire, which flowed like water, and emptied itself into the great sea westwards.

(Enoch 17:5)
I saw every large river, until I arrived at the great darkness. I went to where all of flesh migrate; and I beheld the mountains of the gloom which constitutes winter, and the place from which issues the water in every abyss.

(Enoch 17:6)
I saw also the mouths of all the rivers in the world, and the mouths of the deep.

~ ~ ~

(Enoch 18:1)
Then surveyed the receptacles of all the winds, perceiving that they contributed to adorn the whole creation, and to preserve the foundation of the earth.

(Enoch 18:2)
I surveyed the stone which supports the corners of the earth.

(Enoch 18:3)
I also beheld the four winds, which bear up the earth, and the firmament of heaven.

(Enoch 18:4)
And I beheld the winds occupying the exalted sky.

(Enoch 18:5)
Arising in the midst of heaven and of earth, and constituting the pillars of heaven.

(Enoch 18:6)
I saw the winds which turn the sky, which cause the orb of the sun and of all the stars to set; and over the earth I saw the winds which support the clouds.

(Enoch 18:7)
I saw the path of the angels.

(Enoch 18:8)
I perceived at the extremity of the earth the firmament of heaven above it. Then I passed on towards the south;

(Enoch 18:9)
Where burnt, both by day and night, six mountains formed of glorious stones; three towards the east, and three towards the south.

(Enoch 18:10)
Those which were towards the east were of a variegated stone; one of which was of margarite, and another of antimony. Those towards the south were of a red stone. The middle one reached to heaven like the throne of God; a throne composed of alabaster, the top of which was of sapphire. I saw, too, a blazing fire hanging over all the mountains.

(Enoch 18:11)
And there I saw a place on the other side of an extended territory, where waters were collected.

(Enoch 18:12)
I likewise beheld terrestrial fountains, deep in the fiery columns of heaven.

(Enoch 18:13)
And in the columns of heaven I beheld fires, which descended without number, but neither on high, nor into the deep. Over these fountains also I perceived a place which had neither the firmament of heaven above it, nor the solid ground underneath

it; neither was there water above it, nor anything on wing; but the spot was desolate.

(Enoch 18:14)
And there I beheld seven stars, like great blazing mountains, and like spirits entreating me.

(Enoch 18:15)
Then the angel said, This place, until the consummation of heaven and earth, will be the prison of the stars, and the host of heaven.

(Enoch 18:16)
The stars which roll over fire are those which transgressed the commandment of God before their time arrived; for they came not in their proper season. Therefore, was he offended with them, and bound them, until the period of the consummation of their crimes in the secret year.

~ ~ ~

(Enoch 19:1)
Then Uriel said, Here the angels, who cohabited with women, appointed their leaders;

(Enoch 19:2)
And being numerous in appearance made men profane, and caused them to err; so that they sacrificed to devils as to gods. For in the great day there shall be a judgment, with which they shall be judged, until they are consumed; and their wives also shall be judged, who led astray the angels of heaven that they might salute them.

(Enoch 19:3)
And I, Enoch, I alone saw the likeness of the end of all things. Nor did any human being see it, as I saw it.

~ ~ ~

(Enoch 64:1)
In those days, Noah saw that the earth became inclined, and that destruction approached.

(Enoch 64:2)
Then he lifted up his feet, and went to the ends of the earth, to the dwelling of his great-grandfather Enoch.

(Enoch 64:3)
And Noah cried with a bitter voice, hear me; Hear me; hear me: three times. And he said, Tell me what is transacting on earth; for the earth labors, and is violently shaken. Surely, I shall perish with it.

(Enoch 64:4)
After this there was a great perturbation on earth, and a voice was heard from heaven. I fell down on my face, when my great-grandfather Enoch came and stood by me.

(Enoch 64:5)
He said to me, why have you cried out to me with a bitter cry and lamentation?

(Enoch 64:6)
A commandment has gone forth from the Lord against those

who dwell on the earth, that they may be destroyed; for they know every secret of the angels, every oppressive and secret power of the devils, and every power of those who commit sorcery, as well as of those who make molten images in the whole earth.

(Enoch 64:7)
They know how silver is produced from the dust of the earth, and how on the earth the metallic drop exists; for lead and tin are not produced from earth, as the primary fountain of their production.

(Enoch 64:8)
There is an angel standing on it, and that angel struggles to prevail.

(Enoch 64:9)
Afterwards my great-grandfather Enoch seized me with his hand, raising me up, and saying to me, Go, for I have asked the Lord of spirits respecting this perturbation of the earth; who replied, On account of their impiety have their innumerable judgments been consummated before me. Respecting the moons have they inquired, and they have known that the earth will perish with those who dwell on it, and that to these there will be no place of refuge forever.

(Enoch 64:10)
They have discovered secrets, and they are those who have been judged; but not you, my son. The Lord of spirits knows that you are pure and good, free from the reproach of discovering secrets.

(Enoch 64:11)
He, the holy one, will establish your name in the midst of

the saints, and will preserve you from those who dwell on the earth. He will establish your seed in righteousness, with dominion and great glory; 1 and from your seed shall spring forth righteous and holy men without number forever.

~ ~ ~

(Enoch 2)
Behold, he comes with ten thousands of his saints, to execute judgment on them, and destroy the wicked, and reprove all the carnal for everything which the sinful and ungodly have done, and committed against him.

~ ~ ~

(Enoch 3:1)
All who are in the heavens know what is transacted there.

(Enoch 3:2)
They know that the heavenly luminaries change not their paths; that each rises and sets regularly, everyone at its proper period, without transgressing the commands which they have received. They behold the earth, and understand what is there transacted, from the beginning to the end of it.

(Enoch 3:3)
They see that every work of God is invariable in the period of its appearance. They behold summer and winter: perceiving

that the whole earth is full of water; and that the cloud, the dew, and the rain refresh it.

~ ~ ~

(Enoch 4)
They consider and behold every tree, how it appears to wither, and every leaf to fall off, except of fourteen trees, which are not deciduous; which wait from the old, to the appearance of the new leaf, for two or three winters.

~ ~ ~

(Enoch 5)
Again, they consider the days of summer, that the sun is on it at its very beginning; while you seek for a covered and shady spot on account of the burning sun; while the earth is scorched up with fervid heat, and you become incapable of walking either on the ground or on the rocks in consequence of that heat.

~ ~ ~

(Enoch 6:1)
They consider how the trees, when they put forth their green leaves, become covered, and produce fruit; understanding

everything, and knowing that he who lives forever does all these things for you:

(Enoch 6:2)
That the works at the beginning of every existing year, that all his works, are subservient to him, and invariable; yet as God has appointed, so are all things brought to pass.

(Enoch 6:3)
They see, too, how the seas and the rivers together complete their respective operations:

(Enoch 6:4)
But you endure not patiently, nor fulfill the commandments of the Lord; but you transgress and calumniate his greatness; and malignant are the words in your polluted mouths against his majesty.

(Enoch 6:5)
You withered in heart, no peace shall be to you!

(Enoch 6:6)
Therefore, your days shall you curse, and the years of your lives shall perish; perpetual execration shall be multiplied, and you shall not obtain mercy.

(Enoch 6:7)
In those days, you shall resign your peace with the eternal maledictions of all the righteous, and sinners shall perpetually execrate you;

(Enoch 6:8)
Shall execrate you with the ungodly.

(Enoch 6:9)
The elect shall possess light, joy, and peace; and they shall inherit the earth.

(Enoch 6:10)
But you, you unholy, shall be accursed.

(Enoch 6:11)
Then shall wisdom be given to the elect, all of whom shall live, and not again transgress by impiety or pride; but shall humble themselves, possessing prudence, and shall not repeat transgression.

(Enoch 6:12)
They shall not be condemned the whole period of their lives, nor die in torment and indignation; but the sum of their days shall be completed, and they shall grow old in peace; while the years of their happiness shall be multiplied with joy, and with peace, forever, the whole duration of their existence.

~ ~ ~

(Enoch 65:1)
After this he showed me the angels of punishment, who were prepared to come, and to open all the mighty waters under the earth:

(Enoch 65:2)
That they may be for judgment, and for the destruction of all those who remain and dwell on the earth.

(Enoch 65:3)
And the Lord of spirits commanded the angels who went forth, not to take up the men and preserve them.

(Enoch 65:4)
For those angels presided over all the mighty waters. Then I went out from the presence of Enoch.

~ ~ ~

(Genesis 6:6)

And it repented the Lord that he had made man on the earth, and it grieved him at his heart.

(Genesis 6:7) (Jasher 4:19) (Jubilees 5:4)

And the Lord said, I will destroy man whom I have created from the face of the earth; both man, and beast, and the creeping thing, and the birds of the air; for I repent that I have made them.

(Jasher 4:20, 5:5)
And all men who walked in the ways of the Lord, died in those days, before the Lord brought the evil on man which He had declared, for this was from the Lord, that they should not see the evil which the Lord spoke of concerning the sons of men.

(Genesis 6:8) (Jasher 4:21) (Jubilees 5:5)

But Noah found grace in the eyes of the Lord; and the Lord chose him and his children to raise up seed from them on the face of the whole earth.

~ ~ ~

(Enoch 66:1)
In those days, the word of God came to me, and said, Noah, behold, your lot has ascended up to me, a lot void of crime, a lot beloved and upright.

(Enoch 66:2)
Now then shall the angels labor at the trees; but when they proceed to this, I will put my hand on it, and preserve it.

(Enoch 66:3)
The seed of life shall arise from it, and a change shall take place, that the dry land may not be left empty. I will establish your seed before me forever and ever, and the seed of those who dwell with you on the surface of the earth. It shall be blessed and multiplied in the presence of the earth, in the name of the Lord.

(Enoch 66:4)
And they shall confine those angels who disclosed impiety. In that burning valley it is, that they shall be confined, which at first my great-grandfather Enoch showed me in the west, where there were mountains of gold and silver, of iron, of fluid metal, and of tin.

(Enoch 66:5)
I beheld that valley in which there was great perturbation, and where the waters were troubled.

(Enoch 66:6)
And when all this was effected, from the fluid mass of fire, and the perturbation which prevailed in that place, there arose a

strong smell of sulphur, which became mixed with the waters; and the valley of the angels, who had been guilty of seduction, burned underneath its soil.

(Enoch 66:7)
Through that valley also rivers of fire were flowing, to which those angels shall be condemned, who seduced the inhabitants of the earth.

(Enoch 66:8)
And in those days, these waters shall be to kings, to princes, to the exalted, and to the inhabitants of the earth, for the healing of the soul and body, and for the judgment of the spirit.

(Enoch 66:9)
Their spirits shall be full of revelry, that they may be judged in their bodies; because they have denied the Lord of spirits, and although they perceive their condemnation day by day, they believe not in his name.

(Enoch 66:10)
And as the inflammation of their bodies shall be great, so shall their spirits undergo a change forever.

(Enoch 66:11)
For no word which is uttered before the Lord of spirits shall be in vain.

(Enoch 66:12)
Judgment has come on them, because they trusted in their carnal revelry, and denied the Lord of spirits.

(Enoch 66:13)
In those days, the waters of that valley shall be changed; for

when the angels shall be judged, then shall the heat of those springs of water experience an alteration.

(Enoch 66:14)
And when the angels shall ascend, the water of the springs shall again undergo a change, and be frozen. Then I heard holy Michael answering and saying, This judgment, with which the angels shall be judged, shall bear testimony against the kings, the princes, and those who possess the earth.

(Enoch 66:15)
For these waters of judgment shall be for their healing, and for the death of their bodies. But they shall not perceive and believe that the waters will be changed, and become a fire, which shall blaze forever.

~ ~ ~

(Enoch 67:1)
After this he gave me the characteristical marks of all the secret things in the book of my great-grandfather Enoch, and in the parables which had been given to him; inserting them for me among the words of the book of parables.

(Enoch 67:2)
At that time, holy Michael answered and said to Raphael, The power of the spirit hurries me away, and impels me on. The severity of the judgment, of the secret judgment of the angels, who is capable of beholding—the endurance of that severe judgment which has taken place and been made permanent—without being melted at the sight of it? Again, holy Michael

answered and said to holy Raphael, Who is there whose heart is not softened by it, and whose reins are not troubled at this thing?

(Enoch 67:3)
Judgment has gone forth against them by those who have thus dragged them away; and that was, when they stood in the presence of the Lord of spirits.

(Enoch 67:4)
In like manner, also holy Rakael said to Raphael, They shall not be before the eye of the Lord; since the Lord of spirits has been offended with them; for like lords have they conducted themselves. Therefore, will he bring on them a secret judgment forever and ever.

(Enoch 67:5)
For neither shall angel nor man receive a portion of it; but they alone shall receive their own judgment forever and ever.

~ ~ ~

(Enoch 68:1)
After this judgment they shall be astonished and irritated; for it shall be exhibited to the inhabitants of the earth.

(Enoch 68:2)
Behold the names of those angels. These are their names. The first of them is Samyaza; the second, Arstikapha: the third, Armen; the fourth, Kakabael; the fifth, Turel; the sixth, Rumyel; the seventh, Danyal; the eighth, Kael; the ninth,

Barakel; the tenth, Azazel; the eleventh, Armers; the twelfth, Bataryal; the thirteenth, Basasael; the fourteenth, Ananel; the fifteenth, Turyal; the sixteenth, Simapiseel; the seventeenth, Yetarel; the eighteenth, Tumael; the nineteenth, Tarel; the twentieth, Rumel; the twenty-first, Azazyel.

(Enoch 68:3)
These are the chiefs of their angels, and the names of the leaders of their hundreds, and the leaders of their fifties, and the leaders of their tens.

(Enoch 68:4)
The name of the first is Yekun: he it was who seduced all the sons of the holy angels; and causing them to descend on earth, led astray the offspring of men.

(Enoch 68:5)
The name of the second is Kesabel, who pointed out evil counsel to the sons of the holy angels, and induced them to corrupt their bodies by generating mankind.

(Enoch 68:6)
The name of the third is Gadrel: he discovered every stroke of death to the children of men.

(Enoch 68:7)
He seduced Eve; and discovered to the children of men the instruments of death, the coat of mail, the shield, and the sword for slaughter; every instrument of death to the children of men.

(Enoch 68:8)
From his hand were these things derived to them who dwell on earth, from that period forever.

(Enoch 68:9)
The name of the fourth is Penemue: he discovered to the children of men bitterness and sweetness;

(Enoch 68:10)
And pointed out to them every secret of their wisdom.

(Enoch 68:11)
He taught men to understand writing, and the use of ink and paper.

(Enoch 68:12)
Therefore, numerous have been those who have gone astray from every period of the world, even to this day.

(Enoch 68:13)
For men were not born for this, thus with pen and with ink to confirm their faith;

(Enoch 68:14)
Since they were not created, except that, like the angels, they might remain righteous and pure.

(Enoch 68:15)
Nor would death, which destroys everything, have affected them;

(Enoch 68:16)
But by this their knowledge they perish, and by this also its power consumes them.

(Enoch 68:17)
The name of the fifth is Kasyade: he discovered to the children of men every wicked stroke of spirits and of demons:

(Enoch 68:18)
The stroke of the embryo in the womb, to diminish it; the stroke of the spirit by the bite of the serpent, and the stroke which is given in the mid-day by the offspring of the serpent, the name of which is Tabaet.

~ ~ ~

(Jasher 5:6)
And after the lapse of many years, in the four hundred and eightieth year of the life of Noah, when all those men, who followed the Lord had died away from among the sons of men, and only Methuselah was then left, God said to Noah and Methuselah, saying,

(Jasher 5:7)
Speak, and proclaim to the sons of men, saying, Thus says the Lord, return from your evil ways and forsake your works, and the Lord will repent of the evil that He declared to do to you, so that it shall not come to pass.

(Jasher 5:8)
For thus says the Lord, Behold I give you a period of one hundred and twenty years; if you will turn to Me and forsake your evil ways, then will I also turn away from the evil which I told you, and it shall not exist, says the Lord.

(Jasher 5:9)
And Noah and Methuselah spoke all the words of the Lord to the sons of men, day after day, constantly speaking to them.

(Jasher 5:10)
But the sons of men would not hearken to them, nor incline their ears to their words, and they were stiffnecked.

(Jasher 5:11)
And the Lord granted them a period of one hundred and twenty years, saying, If they will return, then will God repent of the evil, so as not to destroy the earth.

(Jasher 5:12)
Noah the son of Lamech refrained from taking a wife in those days, to beget children, for he said, Surely now God will destroy the earth, wherefore then shall I beget children?

(Genesis 6:9) (Jasher 5:12)
These are the generations of Noah: Noah was a just man and perfect in his generations, and Noah walked with God. And the Lord chose him to raise up seed from his seed upon the face of the earth.

(Jasher 5:14)
And the Lord said to Noah, Take to you a wife, and beget children, for I have seen you are righteous before Me in this generation.

(Jasher 5:15)
And you shall raise up seed, and your children with you, in the midst of the earth; and Noah went and took a wife, and he chose Naamah the daughter of Enoch, and she was five hundred and eighty years old.

(Jasher 5:16)
And Noah was four hundred and ninety-eight years old, when he took Naamah for a wife.

(Genesis 6:10)
And Noah begot three sons, Shem, Ham, and Japheth.

(Jasher 5:17)
And Naamah conceived and bare a son, and he called his name Japheth, saying, God has enlarged me in the earth; and she conceived again and bare a son, and he called his name Shem, saying, God has made me a remnant, to raise up seed in the midst of the earth.

(Jasher 5:18)
And Noah was five hundred and two years old when Naamah bare Shem, and the boys grew up and went in the ways of the Lord, in all that Methuselah and Noah their father taught them.

(Jasher 5:19)
And Lamech the father of Noah, died in those days; yet verily he did not go with all his heart in the ways of his father, and he died in the hundred and ninety-fifth year of the life of Noah.

(Jasher 5:21)
And all the sons of men who knew the Lord, died in that year before the Lord brought evil upon them; for the Lord willed them to die, so as not to behold the evil that God would bring upon their brothers and relatives, as he had so declared to do.

(Jasher 5:22)
In that time, the Lord said to Noah and Methuselah, Stand forth and proclaim to the sons of men all the words that I spoke to you in those days, peradventure they may turn from their evil ways, and I will then repent of the evil and will not bring it.

(Jasher 5:23)
And Noah and Methuselah stood forth, and said in the ears of the sons of men, all that God had spoken concerning them.

(Jasher 5:24)
But the sons of men would not hearken, neither would they incline their ears to all their declarations.

(Genesis 6:11)
The earth also was corrupt before God, and the earth was filled with violence.

(Genesis 6:12) (Jubilee 5:3)
And God looked on the earth, and, behold, it was corrupt; for all flesh had corrupted his way on the earth, and all that were on the earth had wrought all manner of evil before His eyes.

(Genesis 6:13) (Jasher 5:25) (Jubilee 5:20, 21...)
And it was after this that the Lord God said to Noah, The end of all flesh is come before Me; for the earth is filled with violence through them on account of their evil deeds; and, behold, I will destroy everything which was on the earth, both men and cattle, and beasts, and birds of the air, and that which move on the earth with the earth.

(...Jubilee 5:21)
And He commanded Noah to make him an ark, that he might save himself from the waters of the flood.

(Genesis 6:14) (Jasher 5:26, ...28)
Go to a certain place and make a large ark of gopher wood; rooms shall you make in the ark, and shall pitch it within and without with pitch, and place it in that spot.

(Genesis 6:15) (Jasher 5:27)

And this is the fashion which you shall make it of: The length of the ark shall be three hundred cubits, the width of it fifty cubits, and the height of it thirty cubits.

(Genesis 6:16) (Jasher 5:28...)

A window shall you make to the ark, and in a cubit shall you finish it above; and the door of the ark shall you set in the side thereof; with lower, second, and third stories shall you make it.

(Genesis 6:17) (Jasher 5:29)

And, behold, I, even I, will bring a flood of waters on the earth, to destroy all flesh, wherein is the breath of life, from under heaven; and everything that is in the earth shall die.

(Genesis 6:18)

But with you will I establish My covenant; and you shall come into the ark, you, and your sons, and your wife, and your sons wives with you.

(Genesis 6:19) (Jasher 5:30)

And of every living thing of all flesh, you and your household shall go and gather two couple of every sort and you shall bring them into the ark, to keep them alive with you, to raise up seed from them upon earth; they shall be male and female.

(Genesis 6:20)

Of birds after their kind, and of cattle after their kind, of every creeping thing of the earth after his kind, two of every sort shall come to you, to keep them alive.

(Genesis 6:21) (Jasher 5:31)

And you take to you of all food that is eaten by all the animals, and you shall gather it to you; and it shall be for food for you, and for them.

(Jasher 5:32)
And you shall choose for your sons three maidens, from the daughters of men, and they shall be wives to your sons.

(Jasher 5:33)
And Noah rose up, and he made the ark, in the place where God had commanded him, and Noah did as God had ordered him.

(Jasher 5:34)
In his five hundred and ninety-fifth year Noah commenced to make the ark, and he made the ark in five years, as the Lord had commanded.

(Jasher 5:35)
Then Noah took the three daughters of Eliakim, son of Methuselah, for wives for his sons, as the Lord had commanded Noah.

(Jasher 5:36)
And it was at that time Methuselah the son of Enoch died, nine hundred and sixty years old was he, at his death.

(Jubilee 5:22)
And Noah made the ark in all respects as He commanded him, in the twenty-seventh jubilee of years, in the fifth week in the fifth year, on the new moon of the first month.

(Genesis 6:22)
Thus, Noah did; according to all that God commanded him, so he did.

Genesis: Chapter Seven

(Genesis 7:1) (Jasher 6:1)

And at that time, after the death of Methuselah, the Lord said to Noah, Come, you and all your house, into the ark; for you have I seen righteous before Me in this generation. Behold I will gather to you all the animals of the earth, the beasts of the field and the birds of the air, and they shall all come and surround the ark.

(Genesis 7:2)

Of every clean beast you shall take to you by sevens, the male and his female: and of beasts that are not clean by two, the male and his female.

(Genesis 7:3)

Of birds also of the air by sevens, the male and the female; to keep seed alive on the face of all the earth.

(Genesis 7:4)

For yet seven days, and I will cause it to rain on the earth forty days and forty nights; and every living substance that I have made will I destroy from off the face of the earth.

(Jasher 6:2)

And you shall go and seat yourself by the doors of the ark, and all the beasts, the animals, and the birds, shall assemble and place themselves before you, and such of them as shall come and crouch before you, shall you take and deliver into the hands of your sons, who shall bring them to the ark, and all that will stand before you shall leave.

(Jasher 6:3)
And the Lord brought this about on the next day, and animals, beasts and birds came in great multitudes and surrounded the ark.

(Jasher 6:4)
And Noah went and seated himself by the door of the ark, and of all flesh that crouched before him, he brought into the ark, and all that stood before him he left upon earth.

(Jasher 6:5)
And a lioness came, with her two whelps, male and female, and the three crouched before Noah, and the two whelps rose up against the lioness and smote her, and made her flee from her place, and she went away, and they returned to their places, and crouched upon the earth before Noah.

(Jasher 6:6)
And the lioness ran away, and stood in the place of the lions.

(Jasher 6:7)
And Noah saw this, and wondered greatly, and he rose and took the two whelps, and brought them into the ark.

(Jasher 6:8)
And Noah brought into the ark from all living creatures that were upon earth, so that there was none left but which Noah brought into the ark.

(Jasher 6:9)
Two and two came to Noah into the ark, but from the clean animals, and clean birds, he brought seven couples, as God had commanded him.

(Jasher 6:10)
And all the animals, and beasts, and birds, were still there, and they surrounded the ark at every place, and the rain had not descended till seven days after.

(Jasher 6:11)
And on that day, the Lord caused the whole earth to shake, and the sun darkened, and the foundations of the world raged, and the whole earth was moved violently, and the lightning flashed, and the thunder roared, and all the fountains in the earth were broken up, such as was not known to the inhabitants before; and God did this mighty act, in order to terrify the sons of men, that there might be no more evil upon earth.

(Jasher 6:12)
And still the sons of men would not return from their evil ways, and they increased the anger of the Lord at that time, and did not even direct their hearts to all this.

~ ~ ~

(Enoch 53:1)
Then I looked and turned myself to another part of the earth, where I beheld a deep valley burning with fire.

(Enoch 53:2)
To this valley they brought monarchs and the mighty.

(Enoch 53:3)
And there my eyes beheld the instruments which they were making, fetters of iron without weight.

(Enoch 53:4)
Then I inquired of the angel of peace, who proceeded with me, saying, For whom are these fetters and instruments prepared?

(Enoch 53:5)
He replied, These are prepared for the host of Azazeel, that they may be delivered over and adjudged to the lowest condemnation; and that their angels may be overwhelmed with hurled stones, as the Lord of spirits has commanded.

(Enoch 53:6)
Michael and Gabriel, Raphael and Phanuel shall be strengthened in that day, and shall then cast them into a furnace of blazing fire, that the Lord of spirits may be avenged of them for their crimes; because they became ministers of Satan, and seduced those who dwell upon earth.

(Enoch 53:7)
In those days shall punishment go forth from the Lord of spirits; and the receptacles of water which are above the heavens shall be opened, and the fountains likewise, which are under the heavens and under the earth.

(Enoch 53:8)
All the waters, which are in the heavens and above them, shall be mixed together.

(Enoch 53:9)
The water which is above heaven shall be the agent;

(Enoch 53:10)
And the water which is under the earth shall be the recipient: and all shall be destroyed who dwell upon earth, and who

dwell under the extremities of heaven.

(Enoch 53:11)
By these means shall they understand the iniquity which they have committed on earth: and by these means shall they perish.

~ ~ ~

(Genesis 7:5)
And Noah did according to all that the Lord commanded him.

(Genesis 7:6)
And Noah was six hundred years old when the flood of waters was on the earth.

(Genesis 7:7) (Jubilees 5:23...)
And Noah went in, in the sixth year thereof, in the second month, on the new moon of the second month, till the sixteenth; and he entered, and all that we brought to him, and his sons, and his wife, and his sons wives with him, into the ark, because of the waters of the flood.

(Genesis 7:8)
Of clean beasts, and of beasts that are not clean, and of birds, and of everything that creeps on the earth.

(Genesis 7:9)
There went in two and two to Noah into the ark, the male and the female, as God had commanded Noah.

(Genesis 7:10) (Jasher 6:13...)

And it came to pass after seven days, that the waters of the flood were on the earth.

(Genesis 7:11) (...Jasher 6:13, 14...) (...Jubilees 5:23, 24)

In the six hundredth year of Noah's life, in the second month, the seventeenth day of the month, at evening, the Lord closed the ark from without. The same day, the mouths of all the fountains of the great deep were broken up, and the Lord opened the seven flood-gates, the windows of heaven, seven mouths in number.

(Genesis 7:12) (...Jasher 6:14) (Jubilees 5:25)

And the flood-gates began to pour down water from the heaven, and the rain was on the earth forty days and forty nights. And the fountains of the deep also sent up waters, until the whole world was full of water.

(Genesis 7:13)

In the selfsame day entered Noah, and Shem, and Ham, and Japheth, the sons of Noah, and Noah's wife, and the three wives of his sons with them, into the ark;

(Genesis 7:14)

They, and every beast after his kind, and all the cattle after their kind, and every creeping thing that creeps on the earth after his kind, and every birds after his kind, every bird of every sort.

(Genesis 7:15)

And they went in to Noah into the ark, two and two of all flesh, wherein is the breath of life.

(Genesis 7:16) (Jasher 6:15)
And they that went in, Noah and his household, and all the living creatures that were with him, went into the ark on account of the waters of the flood, male and female of all flesh, as God had commanded him: and the Lord shut him in.

(Jasher 6:16)
And all the sons of men that were left upon the earth, became exhausted through evil on account of the rain, for the waters were coming more violently upon the earth, and the animals and beasts were still surrounding the ark.

(Jasher 6:17)
And the sons of men assembled together, about seven hundred thousand men and women, and they came to Noah to the ark.

(Jasher 6:18)
And they called to Noah, saying, Open for us that we may come to you in the ark -- and wherefore shall we die?

(Jasher 6:19)
And Noah, with a loud voice, answered them from the ark, saying, Have you not all rebelled against the Lord, and said that He does not exist? And therefore the Lord brought upon you this evil, to destroy and cut you off from the face of the earth.

(Jasher 6:20)
Is not this the thing that I spoke to you of one hundred and twenty years back, and you would not hearken to the voice of the Lord, and now do you desire to live upon earth?

(Jasher 6:21)
And they said to Noah, We are ready to return to the Lord;

only open for us that we may live and not die.

(Jasher 6:22)
And Noah answered them, saying, Behold now that you see the trouble of your souls, you wish to return to the Lord; why did you not return during these hundred and twenty years, which the Lord granted you as the determined period?

(Jasher 6:23)
But now you come and tell me this on account of the troubles of your souls, now also the Lord will not listen to you, neither will He give ear to you on this day, so that you will not now succeed in your wishes.

(Jasher 6:24)
And the sons of men approached in order to break into the ark, to come in on account of the rain, for they could not bear the rain upon them.

(Jasher 6:25)
And the Lord sent all the beasts and animals that stood round the ark. And the beasts overpowered them and drove them from that place, and every man went his way and they again scattered themselves upon the face of the earth.

(Jubilees 5:19)
And as for all those who corrupted their ways and their thoughts before the flood, no man's person was accepted save that of Noah alone; for his person was accepted in behalf of his sons, whom God saved from the waters of the flood on his account; for his heart was righteous in all his ways, according as it was commanded regarding him, and he had not departed from aught that was ordained for him.

(Genesis 7:17) (Jasher 6:27) (Jubilees 6:26...)

And the flood was forty days on the earth; And the waters prevailed and they greatly increased upon the earth and the waters increased, and bore up the ark, and it was lift up above the earth. And it moved on the face of the waters.

(Genesis 7:18) (Jasher 6:26...)

And the rain was still descending upon the earth, and it descended forty days and forty nights, and the waters prevailed, and were increased greatly on the earth; and the ark went on the face of the waters.

(Genesis 7:19)

And the waters prevailed exceedingly on the earth; and all the high hills, that were under the whole heaven, were covered.

(Genesis 7:20) (...Jubilees 6:26)

And the waters increased on the earth: fifteen cubits upward the waters prevailed and rose above all the high mountains; the mountains were covered.

~ ~ ~

(Enoch 57:1)

In those days, my eyes beheld the secrets of the lightnings and the splendors, and the judgment belonging to them.

(Enoch 57:2)

They lighten for a blessing and for a curse, according to the will of the Lord of spirits.

(Enoch 57:3)
And there I saw the secrets of the thunder, when it rattles above in heaven, and its sound is heard.

(Enoch 57:4)
The habitations also of the earth were shown to me. The sound of the thunder is for peace and for blessing, as well as for a curse, according to the word of the Lord of spirits.

(Enoch 57:5)
Afterwards every secret of the splendors and of the lightnings was seen by me. For blessing and for fertility they lighten.

~ ~ ~

(Genesis 7:21) (...Jasher 6:26...)
And all flesh died that moved on the earth, both of birds, and of cattle, and of beast, and of every creeping thing that creeps on the earth, and every man:

(Genesis 7:22)
All in whose nostrils was the breath of life, of all that was in the dry land, died.

(Genesis 7:23) (...Jasher 6:26)
And every living substance was destroyed which was on the face of the ground, both man, and cattle, and the creeping things, and the birds of the heaven; and they were destroyed from the earth: and Noah only remained alive, and they that were with him in the ark.

(Genesis 7:24) (Jubilees 6:27)
And the waters prevailed on the earth five months - a hundred and fifty days.

(Jasher 6:28)
And the ark floated upon the face of the waters, and it was tossed upon the waters so that all the living creatures within were turned about like pottage in a cauldron.

(Jasher 6:29)
And great anxiety seized all the living creatures that were in the ark, and the ark was like to be broken.

(Jasher 6:30)
And all the living creatures that were in the ark were terrified, and the lions roared, and the oxen lowed, and the wolves howled, and every living creature in the ark spoke and lamented in its own language, so that their voices reached to a great distance, and Noah and his sons cried and wept in their troubles; they were greatly afraid that they had reached the gates of death.

(Jasher 6:31)
And Noah prayed to the Lord, and cried to him on account of this, and he said, O Lord help us, for we have no strength to bear this evil that has encompassed us, for the waves of the waters have surrounded us, mischievous torrents have terrified us, the snares of death have come before us; answer us, O Lord, answer us, light up your countenance toward us and be gracious to us, redeem us and deliver us.

Genesis: Chapter Eight

(Genesis 8:1) (Jasher 6:32, 33)

And the Lord hearkened to the voice of Noah. And the Lord God remembered Noah, and every living thing, and all the cattle that was with him in the ark: and God made a wind to pass over the earth, and the waters subsided; and the waters were still and the ark rested.

(Genesis 8:2) (Jasher 6:34)

The fountains also of the deep and the windows of heaven were stopped, and the rain from heaven was restrained;

(Genesis 8:3) (Jasher 6:35...)

And the waters decreased in those days and returned from off the earth continually: and after the end of the hundred and fifty days the waters were abated.

(Genesis 8:4) (...Jasher 6:35) (Jubilees 6:28)

And the ark rested in the seventh month, on the seventeenth day of the month, on the top of Lubar, one of the mountains of Ararat.

(Jasher 6:36)

And Noah then opened the windows of the ark, and Noah still called out to the Lord at that time and he said, O Lord, who formed the earth and the heavens and all that are therein, bring forth our souls from this confinement, and from the prison wherein You have placed us, for I am much wearied with sighing.

(Jasher 6:37)
And the Lord hearkened to the voice of Noah, and said to him, When you have completed a full year, then you shall go forth.

(Jubilees 6:29)
And on the new moon in the fourth month the fountains of the great deep were closed and the flood-gates of heaven were restrained; and on the new moon of the seventh month all the mouths of the abysses of the earth were opened, and the water began to descend into the deep below.

(Genesis 8:5) (Jubilees 6:30...)
And the waters decreased continually until the tenth month: in the tenth month, on the first day of the month, the tops of the mountains were seen.

(Genesis 8:6)
And it came to pass at the end of forty days, that Noah opened the window of the ark which he had made:

(Genesis 8:7)
And he sent forth a raven, which went forth to and fro, until the waters were dried up from off the earth.

(Genesis 8:8)
Also, he sent forth a dove from him, to see if the waters were abated from off the face of the ground;

(Genesis 8:9)
But the dove found no rest for the sole of her foot, and she returned to him into the ark, for the waters were on the face of the whole earth: then he put forth his hand, and took her, and pulled her in to him into the ark.

(Genesis 8:10)

And he stayed yet other seven days; and again, he sent forth the dove out of the ark;

(Genesis 8:11)

And the dove came in to him in the evening; and, lo, in her mouth was an olive leaf plucked off: so Noah knew that the waters were abated from off the earth.

(Genesis 8:12)

And he stayed yet other seven days; and sent forth the dove; which returned not again to him anymore.

(Genesis 8:13) (Jasher 6:38) (...Jubilees 6:30)

And it came to pass in the six hundredth and first year, in the first month, the first day of the month, at the revolution of the year, when a full year was completed to Noah's dwelling in the ark, the waters were dried up from off the earth: and the earth became visible and Noah removed the covering of the ark, and looked, and, behold, the face of the ground was dry.

(Jubilees 6:31)
And the waters disappeared from above the earth in the fifth week in the seventh year thereof, and on the seventeenth day in the second month the earth was dry.

(Genesis 8:14) (Jasher 6:39) (Jubilees 6:32)

And at that time in the second month, on the twenty-seventh day of the month, the earth was dried; he opened the ark, and sent forth from it beasts, and cattle, and birds, and every moving thing but Noah and his sons, and those that were with him, did not go out from the ark until the Lord told them.

(Genesis 8:15) (Jasher 6:40...)
And the day came that the Lord God spoke to Noah, saying,

(Genesis 8:16) (...Jasher 6:40...)
Go forth of the ark, you, and your wife, and your sons, and your sons wives with you.

(Genesis 8:17)
Bring forth with you every living thing that is with you, of all flesh, both of birds, and of cattle, and of every creeping thing that creeps on the earth; that they may breed abundantly in the earth, and be fruitful, and multiply on the earth.

(Genesis 8:18) (...Jasher 6:40) (Jubilees 6:1...)
And on the new moon of the third month Noah went forth, and his sons, and his wife, and his sons wives with him: they all went out from the ark.

(Genesis 8:19)
Every beast, every creeping thing, and every bird, and whatsoever creeps on the earth, after their kinds, went forth out of the ark.

(Jasher 6:41)
And they went and everyone returned to his way and to his place, and Noah and his sons dwelt in the land that God had told them, and they served the Lord all their days, and the Lord blessed Noah and his sons on their going out from the ark.

(Genesis 8:20) (...Jubilees 6:1)
And Noah built an altar to the Lord on that mountain; and took of every clean beast, and of every clean bird, and offered burnt offerings on the altar.

(Jubilees 6:2)
And he made atonement for the earth, and took a kid and made atonement by its blood for all the guilt of the earth; for everything that had been on it had been destroyed, save those that were in the ark with Noah.

(Jubilees 6:3)
And he placed the fat thereof on the altar, and he took an ox, and a goat, and a sheep and kids, and salt, and a turtle-dove, and the young of a dove, and placed a burnt sacrifice on the altar, and poured thereon an offering mingled with oil, and sprinkled wine and strewed frankincense over everything, and caused a goodly savor to arise, acceptable before the Lord.

(Genesis 8:21) (Jubilees 6:4…)
And the Lord smelled a sweet savor; and the Lord said in his heart, I will not again curse the ground any more for man's sake; for the imagination of man's heart is evil from his youth; neither will I again smite any more everything living, as I have done.

(…Jubilees 6:4…)
And He made a covenant with him that there should not be any more a flood to destroy the earth;

(Genesis 8:22) (…Jubilees 6:4)
While the earth remains, seedtime and harvest, and cold and heat, and summer and winter, and day and night shall not change their order nor cease.

Genesis: Chapter Nine

(Genesis 9:1) (Jasher 6:42) (Jubilees 6:5...)

And God blessed Noah and his sons, and said to them, Be fruitful, and fill all the earth, become strong and increase abundantly in the earth and multiply therein, and replenish the earth, and become many on it, and be a blessing on it.

(Genesis 9:2) (...Jubilees 6:5)

And the fear of you and the dread of you shall be on every beast of the earth, and on every bird of the air, on all that moves on the earth, and on all the fishes of the sea; into your hand are they delivered.

(Genesis 9:3) (Jubilees 6:6)

And behold I have given to you all beasts, and all winged things, and everything that moves on the earth, and the fish in the waters, and every moving thing that lives shall be meat for you; even as the green herb have I given you all things to eat.

(Genesis 9:4) (Jubilees 6:7...)

But flesh with the life thereof, which is the blood thereof, you shall not eat; for the life of all flesh is in the blood.

(Genesis 9:5) (...Jubilees 6:7)

And surely your blood of your lives will I require; at the hand of every beast will I require it, and at the hand of man; at the hand of every man's brother will I require the life of man.

(Genesis 9:6) (Jubilees 6:8)

Whoso sheds man's blood, by man shall his blood be shed: for in the image of God, He made man.

(Genesis 9:7) (Jubilees 6:9)
And you, be fruitful, and multiply; bring forth abundantly in the earth, and multiply therein.

(Jubilees 6:10)
And Noah and his sons swore that they would not eat any blood that was in any flesh, and he made a covenant before the Lord God forever throughout all the generations of the earth in this month.

(Jubilees 6:11)
On this account, He spoke to you that you should make a covenant with the children of Israel in this month on the mountain with an oath, and that you should sprinkle blood on them because of all the words of the covenant, which the Lord made with them forever.

(Jubilees 6:12)
And this testimony is written concerning you that you should observe it continually, so that you should not eat on any day any blood of beasts or birds or cattle during all the days of the earth, and the man who eats the blood of beast or of cattle or of birds during all the days of the earth, he and his seed shall be rooted out of the land.

(Jubilees 6:13)
And command the children of Israel to eat no blood, so that their names and their seed may be before the Lord our God continually.

(Jubilees 6:14)
And for this law there is no limit of days, for it is forever. They

shall observe it throughout their generations, so that they may continue supplicating on your behalf with blood before the altar; every day and at the time of morning and evening they shall seek forgiveness on your behalf perpetually before the Lord that they may keep it and not be rooted out.

~ ~ ~

(Enoch 54:1)
Afterwards the Ancient of Days repented, and said, In vain have I destroyed all the inhabitants of the earth.

(Enoch 54:2)
And he swore by his great name, saying, From here on out, I will not act thus towards all those who dwell upon earth.

(Enoch 54:3)
But I will place a sign in the heavens; and it shall be a faithful witness between me and them forever, as long as the days of heaven and earth last upon the earth.

(Enoch 54:4)
Afterwards, according to this my decree, when I shall be disposed to seize them beforehand, by the instrumentality of angels, in the day of affliction and trouble, my wrath and my punishment shall remain upon them, my punishment and my wrath, says God the Lord of spirits.

(Enoch 54:5)
O you kings, O you mighty, who inhabit the world, you shall behold my Elect One, sitting upon the throne of my glory. And

he shall judge Azazeel, all his associates, and all his hosts, in the name of the Lord of spirits.

(Enoch 54:6)
There likewise I beheld hosts of angels who were moving in punishment, confined in a net-work of iron and brass. Then I inquired of the angel of peace, who proceeded with me, to whom those under confinement were going.

(Enoch 54:7)
He said, To each of their elect and their beloved, that they may be cast into the fountains and deep recesses of the valley.

(Enoch 54:8)
And that valley shall be filled with their elect and beloved; the days of whose life shall be consumed, but the days of their error shall be innumerable.

(Enoch 54:9)
Then shall princes combine together, and conspire. The chiefs of the east, among the Parthians and Medes, shall remove kings, in whom a spirit of perturbation shall enter. They shall hurl them from their thrones, springing as lions from their dens, and like famished wolves into the midst of the flock.

(Enoch 54:10)
They shall go up, and tread upon the land of their elect. The land of their elect shall be before them. The threshing-floor, the path, and the city of my righteous people shall impede the progress of their horses. They shall rise up to destroy each other; their right hand shall be strengthened; nor shall a man acknowledge his friend or his brother;

(Enoch 54:11)
Nor the son his father and his mother; until the number of the dead bodies shall be completed, by their death and punishment. Neither shall this take place without cause.

(Enoch 54:12)
In those days shall the mouth of hell be opened, into which they shall be immerged; hell shall destroy and swallow up sinners from the face of the elect.

~ ~ ~

(Enoch 55:1)
After this I beheld another army of chariots, with men riding in them.

(Enoch 55:2)
And they came upon the wind from the east, from the west, and from the south.

(Enoch 55:3)
The sound of the noise of their chariots was heard.

(Enoch 55:4)
And when that agitation took place, the saints out of heaven perceived it; the pillar of the earth shook from its foundation; and the sound was heard from the extremities of the earth to the extremities of heaven at the same time.

(Enoch 55:5)
Then they all fell down, and worshipped the Lord of spirits.

(Enoch 55:6)
This is the end of the second parable.

~ ~ ~

(Genesis 9:8)
And God spoke to Noah, and to his sons with him, saying,

(Genesis 9:9)
And I, behold, I establish My covenant with you, and with your seed after you;

(Genesis 9:10)
And with every living creature that is with you, of the birds, of the cattle, and of every beast of the earth with you; from all that go out of the ark, to every beast of the earth.

(Genesis 9:11)
And I will establish My covenant with you; neither shall all flesh be cut off any more by the waters of a flood; neither shall there anymore be a flood to destroy the earth.

(Genesis 9:12)
And God said, This is the token of the covenant which I make between Me and you and every living creature that is with you, for perpetual generations:

(Genesis 9:13)
I do set My bow in the cloud, and it shall be for a token of a covenant between Me and the earth.

(Genesis 9:14)
And it shall come to pass, when I bring a cloud over the earth, that the bow shall be seen in the cloud:

(Genesis 9:15)
And I will remember My covenant, which is between Me and you and every living creature of all flesh; and the waters shall no more become a flood to destroy all flesh.

(Genesis 9:16)
And the bow shall be in the cloud; and I will look on it, that I may remember the everlasting covenant between God and every living creature of all flesh that is on the earth.

(Jubilees 6:15)
And He gave to Noah and his sons a sign that there should not again be a flood on the earth.

(Jubilees 6:16)
He set His bow in the cloud for a sign of the eternal covenant that there should not again be a flood on the earth to destroy it all the days of the earth.

(Jubilees 6:17)
For this reason, it is ordained and written on the heavenly tablets, that they should celebrate the feast of weeks in this month once a year, to renew the covenant every year.

(Jubilees 6:18)
And this whole festival was celebrated in heaven from the day of creation till the days of Noah - twenty-six jubilees and five weeks of years: and Noah and his sons observed it for seven jubilees and one week of years, till the day of Noah's death,

and from the day of Noah's death his sons did away with it until the days of Abraham, and they eat blood.

(Jubilees 6:19)
But Abraham observed it, and Isaac and Jacob and his children observed it up to your days, and in your days the children of Israel forgot it until you celebrated it anew on this mountain.

(Jubilees 6:20)
And command the children of Israel to observe this festival in all their generations for a commandment to them: one day in the year in this month they shall celebrate the festival.

(Jubilees 6:21)
For it is the feast of weeks and the feast of first fruits: this feast is twofold and of a double nature: according to what is written and engraved concerning it, celebrate it.

(Jubilees 6:22)
For I have written in the book of the first law, in that which I have written for you, that you should celebrate it in its season, one day in the year, and I explained to you its sacrifices that the children of Israel should remember and should celebrate it throughout their generations in this month, one day in every year.

(Jubilees 6:23)
And on the new moon of the first month, and on the new moon of the fourth month, and on the new moon of the seventh month, and on the new moon of the tenth month are the days of remembrance, and the days of the seasons in the four divisions of the year. These are written and ordained as a testimony forever.

(Jubilees 6:24)
And Noah ordained them for himself as feasts for the generations forever, so that they have become thereby a memorial to him.

(Jubilees 6:25)
And on the new moon of the first month he was bidden to make for himself an ark, and on that day the earth became dry and he opened the ark and saw the earth.

(Jubilees 6:26)
And on the new moon of the fourth month the mouths of the depths of the abyss beneath were closed. And on the new moon of the seventh month all the mouths of the abysses of the earth were opened, and the waters began to descend into them.

(Jubilees 6:27)
And on the new moon of the tenth month the tops of the mountains were seen, and Noah was glad.

(Jubilees 6:28)
And on this account, he ordained them for himself as feasts for a memorial forever, and thus are they ordained.

(Jubilees 6:29)
And they placed them on the heavenly tablets, each had thirteen weeks; from one to another their memorial, from the first to the second, and from the second to the third, and from the third to the fourth.

(Jubilees 6:30)
And all the days of the commandment will be two and fifty weeks of days, and these will make the entire year complete.

Thus it is engraved and ordained on the heavenly tablets.

(Jubilees 6:31)
And there is no neglecting this commandment for a single year or from year to year.

(Jubilees 6:32)
And command you the children of Israel that they observe the years according to this reckoning- three hundred and sixty-four days, and these will constitute a complete year, and they will not disturb its time from its days and from its feasts; for everything will fall out in them according to their testimony, and they will not leave out any day nor disturb any feasts.

(Jubilees 6:33)
But if they do neglect and do not observe them according to His commandment, then they will disturb all their seasons and the years will be dislodged from this, and they will disturb the seasons and the years will be dislodged and they will neglect their ordinances.

(Jubilees 6:34)
And all the children of Israel will forget and will not find the path of the years, and will forget the new moons, and seasons, and sabbaths and they will go wrong as to all the order of the years.

(Jubilees 6:35)
For I know and from here after, I will declare it to you, and it is not of my own devising; for the book, written before me, and on the heavenly tablets the division of days is ordained, lest they forget the feasts of the covenant and walk according to the feasts of the Gentiles after their error and after their ignorance.

(Jubilees 6:36)
For there will be those who will assuredly make observations of the moon -how it disturbs the seasons and comes in from year to year ten days too soon.

(Jubilees 6:37)
For this reason, the years will come on them when they will disturb the order, and make an abominable day the day of testimony, and an unclean day a feast day, and they will confound all the days, the holy with the unclean, and the unclean day with the holy; for they will go wrong as to the months and sabbaths and feasts and jubilees.

(Jubilees 6:38)
For this reason, I command and testify to you that you may testify to them; for after your death your children will disturb them, so that they will not make the year three hundred and sixty-four days only, and for this reason they will go wrong as to the new moons and seasons and sabbaths and festivals, and they will eat all kinds of blood with all kinds of flesh.

(Genesis 9:17)

And God said to Noah, This is the token of the covenant, which I have established between Me and all flesh that is on the earth.

(Genesis 9:18)

And the sons of Noah, that went forth of the ark, were Shem, and Ham, and Japheth: and Ham is the father of Canaan.

(Genesis 9:19)

These are the three sons of Noah: and of them was the whole earth overspread.

~ ~ ~

(Enoch 56:1)
Now began to utter the third parable, concerning the saints and the elect.

(Enoch 56:2)
Blessed are you, O saints and elect, for glorious is your lot.

(Enoch 56:3)
The saints shall exist in the light of the sun, and the elect in the light of everlasting life, the days of whose life shall never terminate; nor shall the days of the saints be numbered, who seek for light, and obtain righteousness with the Lord of spirits.

(Enoch 56:4)
Peace be to the saints with the Lord of the world.

(Enoch 56:5)
From here on out, the saints shall be told to seek in heaven the secrets of righteousness, the portion of faith; for like the sun has it arisen upon the earth, while darkness has passed away. There shall be light interminable: nor shall they enter upon the enumeration of time; for darkness shall be previously destroyed, and light shall increase before the Lord of spirits; before the Lord of spirits shall the light of uprightness increase forever.

~ ~ ~

(Genesis 9:20) (Jubilees 7:1)
And Noah began to be a husbandman, and in the seventh week in the first year thereof, in this jubilee, Noah planted a vineyard on the mountain on which the ark had rested, named Lubar, one of the Ararat Mountains, and they produced fruit in the fourth year, and he guarded their fruit, and gathered it in this year in the seventh month.

(Jubilees 7:2)
And he made wine therefrom and put it into a vessel, and kept it until the fifth year, until the first day, on the new moon of the first month.

(Jubilees 7:3)
And he celebrated with joy the day of this feast, and he made a burnt sacrifice to the Lord, one young ox and one ram, and seven sheep, each a year old, and a kid of the goats, that he might make atonement thereby for himself and his sons.

(Jubilees 7:4)
And he prepared the kid first, and placed some of its blood on the flesh that was on the altar which he had made, and all the fat he laid on the altar where he made the burnt sacrifice, and the ox and the ram and the sheep, and he laid all their flesh on the altar.

(Jubilees 7:5)
And he placed all their offerings mingled with oil on it, and afterwards he sprinkled wine on the fire which he had previously made on the altar, and he placed incense on the altar and caused a sweet savor to ascend acceptable before the Lord his God.

(Genesis 9:21) (Jubilees 7:6,7)
And he rejoiced and drank of the wine, he and his children with joy. And it was evening, and he went into his tent, and was drunk; he lay down and slept and he was uncovered within his tent as he slept.

(Genesis 9:22) (Jubilees 7:8)
And Ham, the father of Canaan, saw the nakedness of Noah his father, and went forth and told his two brothers without.

(Genesis 9:23) (Jubilees 7:9)
And Shem and Japheth took a garment and arose, and laid it on both their shoulders, and went backward, and covered the nakedness of their father; and their faces were backward, and they saw not their father's nakedness.

(Genesis 9:24) (Jubilees 7:10...)
And Noah awoke from his wine, and knew what his younger son had done to him.

(Genesis 9:25) (...Jubilees 7:10)
And he said, Cursed be Canaan; a servant of servants shall he be to his brothers.

(Genesis 9:26) (Jubilees 7:11)
And he blessed Shem, and he said, Blessed be the Lord God of Shem; and Canaan shall be his servant.

(Genesis 9:27) (Jubilees 7:12)
God shall enlarge Japheth, and he shall dwell in the tents of Shem; and Canaan shall be his servant.

(Genesis 9:28)
And Noah lived after the flood three hundred and fifty years.

(Jubilees 7:13)
And Ham knew that his father had cursed his younger son, and he was displeased that he had cursed his son. And he parted from his father, he and his sons with him, Cush and Mizraim and Put and Canaan.

(Jubilees 7:14)
And he built for himself a city and called its name after the name of his wife Neelatamauk.

(Jubilees 7:15)
And Japheth saw it, and became envious of his brother, and he too built for himself a city, and he called its name after the name of his wife Adataneses.

(Jubilees 7:16)
And Shem dwelt with his father Noah, and he built a city close to his father on the mountain, and he too called its name after the name of his wife Sedeqetelebab.

(Jubilees 7:17)
And behold these three cities are near Mount Lubar; Sedeqetelebab fronting the mountain on its east; and Naeltamauk on the south; Adataneses towards the west.

(Jubilees 7:18)
And these are the sons of Shem: Elam, and Asshur, and Arpachshad - this son was born two years after the flood - and Lud, and Aram.

(Jubilees 7:19)
The sons of Japheth: Gomer and Magog and Madai and Javan, Tubal and Meshech and Tiras: these are the sons of Noah.

(Jubilees 7:20)
And in the twenty-eighth jubilee, Noah began to enjoin on his sons' sons the ordinances and commandments, and all the judgments that he knew, and he exhorted his sons to observe righteousness, and to cover the shame of their flesh, and to bless their Creator, and honor father and mother, and love their neighbor, and guard their souls from fornication and uncleanness and all iniquity.

(Jubilees 7:21)
For owing to these three things came the flood on the earth, namely, owing to the fornication wherein the Watchers against the law of their ordinances went a whoring after the daughters of men, and took themselves wives of all which they chose: and they made the beginning of uncleanness.

(Jubilees 7:22)
And they begot sons the Naphidim, and they were all unlike, and they devoured one another: and the Giants slew the Naphil, and the Naphil slew the Eljo, and the Eljo mankind, and one man another.

(Jubilees 7:23)
And everyone sold himself to work iniquity and to shed much blood, and the earth was filled with iniquity.

(Jubilees 7:24)
And after this they sinned against the beasts and birds, and all that moves and walks on the earth: and much blood was shed on the earth, and every imagination and desire of men imagined vanity and evil continually.

(Jubilees 7:25)
And the Lord destroyed everything from off the face of the

earth; because of the wickedness of their deeds, and because of the blood which they had shed in the midst of the earth He destroyed everything.

(Jubilees 7:26)
And we were left, I and you, my sons, and everything that entered with us into the ark, and behold I see your works before me that you do not walk in righteousness: for in the path of destruction you have begun to walk, and you are parting one from another, and are envious one of another, and so it comes that you are not in harmony, my sons, each with his brother.

(Jubilees 7:27)
For I see, and behold the demons have begun their seductions against you and against your children and now I fear on your behalf, that after my death you will shed the blood of men on the earth, and that you, too, will be destroyed from the face of the earth.

(Jubilees 7:28)
For whoso sheds man's blood, and whoso eats the blood of any flesh, shall all be destroyed from the earth.

(Jubilees 7:29)
And there shall not be left any man that eats blood, or that sheds the blood of man on the earth, Nor shall there be left to him any seed or descendants living under heaven; For into Sheol shall they go, And into the place of condemnation shall they descend, And into the darkness of the deep shall they all be removed by a violent death.

(Jubilees 7:30)
There shall be no blood seen on you of all the blood there shall

be all the days in which you have killed any beasts or cattle or whatever flies on the earth, and work you a good work to your souls by covering that which has been shed on the face of the earth.

(Jubilees 7:31)
And you shall not be like him who eats with blood, but guard yourselves that none may eat blood before you: cover the blood, for thus have I been commanded to testify to you and your children, together with all flesh.

(Jubilees 7:32)
And suffer not the soul to be eaten with the flesh, that your blood, which is your life, may not be required at the hand of any flesh that sheds it on the earth.

(Jubilees 7:33)
For the earth will not be clean from the blood which has been shed on it; for through the blood of him that shed it will the earth be purified throughout all its generations.

(Jubilees 7:34)
And now, my children, harken: work judgment and righteousness that you maybe planted in righteousness over the face of the whole earth, and your glory lifted up before my God, who saved me from the waters of the flood.

(Jubilees 7:35)
And behold, you will go and build for yourselves cities, and plant in them all the plants that are on the earth, and moreover all fruit-bearing trees.

(Jubilees 7:36)
For three years the fruit of everything that is eaten will not

be gathered: and in the fourth year its fruit will be accounted holy and they will offer the first-fruits, acceptable before the Most High God, Who created heaven and earth and all things. Let them offer in abundance the first of the wine and oil as first-fruits on the altar of the Lord, who receives it, and what is left let the servants of the house of the Lord eat before the altar which receives it.

(Jubilees 7:37)
And in the fifth year make you the release so that you release it in righteousness and uprightness, and you shall be righteous, and all that you plant shall prosper.

(Jubilees 7:38)
For thus Enoch, the father of your father, commanded Methuselah, his son, and Methuselah his son Lamech, and Lamech commanded me all the things which his fathers commanded him.

(Jubilees 7:39)
And I also will give you commandment, my sons, as Enoch commanded his son in the first jubilees: while still living, the seventh in his generation, he commanded and testified to his son and to his son's sons until the day of his death.

~ ~ ~

(Jubilees 10:1)
And in the third week of this jubilee the unclean demons began to lead astray the children of the sons of Noah, and to make to err and destroy them.

(Jubilees 10:2)
And the sons of Noah came to Noah their father, and they told him concerning the demons which were leading astray and blinding and slaying his sons' sons.

(Jubilees 10:3)
And he prayed before the Lord his God, and said: God of the spirits of all flesh, who has shown mercy to me and have saved me and my sons from the waters of the flood, and have not caused me to perish as You did the sons of perdition; for Your grace has been great towards me, and great has been Your mercy to my soul; Let Your grace be lift up on my sons, and let not wicked spirits rule over them lest they should destroy them from the earth.

(Jubilees 10:4)
But do You bless me and my sons, that we may increase and Multiply and replenish the earth.

(Jubilees 10:5)
And You know how Your Watchers, the fathers of these spirits, acted in my day: and as for these spirits which are living, imprison them and hold them fast in the place of condemnation, and let them not bring destruction on the sons of your servant, my God; for these are malignant, and created in order to destroy.

(Jubilees 10:6)
And let them not rule over the spirits of the living; for You alone can exercise dominion over them. And let them not have power over the sons of the righteous from here after, and forevermore.

(Jubilees 10:7)
And the Lord our God bade us to bind all.

(Jubilees 10:8)
And the chief of the spirits, Mastêmâ, came and said: Lord, Creator, let some of them remain before me, and let them harken to my voice, and do all that I shall say to them; for if some of them are not left to me, I shall not be able to execute the power of my will on the sons of men; for these are for corruption and leading astray before my judgment, for great is the wickedness of the sons of men.

(Jubilees 10:9)
And He said: Let the tenth part of them remain before him, and let nine parts descend into the place of condemnation.

(Jubilees 10:10)
And one of us He commanded that we should teach Noah all their medicines; for He knew that they would not walk in uprightness, nor strive in righteousness.

(Jubilees 10:11)
And we did according to all His words: all the malignant evil ones we bound in the place of condemnation and a tenth part of them we left that they might be subject before Satan on the earth.

(Jubilees 10:12)
And we explained to Noah all the medicines of their diseases, together with their seductions, how he might heal them with herbs of the earth.

(Jubilees 10:13)
And Noah wrote down all things in a book as we instructed

him concerning every kind of medicine. Thus the evil spirits were precluded from the sons of Noah.

(Jubilees 10:14)
And he gave all that he had written to Shem, his eldest son; for he loved him exceedingly above all his sons.

(Jubilees 10:15)
And Noah slept with his fathers, and was buried on Mount Lubar in the land of Ararat.

(Genesis 9:29) (Jubilees 10:16)
And all the days of Noah were nine hundred and fifty years: he completed in his life, nineteen jubilees and two weeks and five years, and he died.

(Jubilees 10:17)
And in his life on earth he excelled the children of men save Enoch because of the righteousness, wherein he was perfect. For Enoch's office was ordained for a testimony to the generations of the world, so that he should recount all the deeds of generation to generation, till the day of judgment.

Genesis: Chapter Ten

(Genesis 10:1) (Jasher 7:1)

Now these are the generations of the sons of Noah, Shem, Ham, and Japheth: and to them were sons born after the flood, for they had taken wives before the flood.

(Genesis 10:2) (Jasher 7:2)

The sons of Japheth; Gomer, and Magog, and Madai, and Javan, and Tubal, and Meshech, and Tiras, seven sons.

(Genesis 10:3) (Jasher 7:3)

And the sons of Gomer; Ashkenaz, and Riphath, and Togarmah.

(Jasher 7:4)

And the sons of Magog were Elichanaf and Lubal.

(Jasher 7:5)

And the children of Madai were Achon, Zeelo, Chazoni and Lot.

(Genesis 10:4) (Jasher 7:6)

And the sons of Javan; Elishah, and Tarshish, Kittim, and Dodanim.

(Jasher 7:7)

And the sons of Tubal were Ariphi, Kesed and Taari.

(Jasher 7:8)

And the sons of Meshech were Dedon, Zaron and Shebashni.

(Jasher 7:9)
And the sons of Tiras were Benib, Gera, Lupirion and Gilak; these are the sons of Japheth according to their families, and their numbers in those days were about four hundred and sixty men.

(Genesis 10:5)
By these were the isles of the Gentiles divided in their lands; everyone after his tongue, after their families, in their nations.

(Genesis 10:6) (Jasher 7:10...)
And these are the sons of Ham; Cush, and Mizraim, and Phut, and Canaan, four sons;

(Genesis 10:7) (...Jasher 7:10)
And the sons of Cush; Seba, and Havilah, and Sabtah, and Raamah, and Sabtecha: and the sons of Raamah; were Sheba, and Dedan.

(Genesis 10:8) (Jasher 7:23)
And Cush the son of Ham, the son of Noah, took a wife in those days in his old age, and she bare a son, and they called his name Nimrod: saying, At that time the sons of men again began to rebel and transgress against God, and the child grew up, and his father loved him exceedingly, for he was the son of his old age. Nimrod began to be a mighty one in the earth.

(Jasher 7:24)
And the garments of skin which God made for Adam and his wife, when they went out of the garden, were given to Cush.

(Jasher 7:25)
For after the death of Adam and his wife, the garments were given to Enoch, the son of Jared, and when Enoch was taken

up to God, he gave them to Methuselah, his son.

(Jasher 7:26)
And at the death of Methuselah, Noah took them and brought them to the ark, and they were with him until he went out of the ark.

(Jasher 7:27)
And in their going out, Ham stole those garments from Noah his father, and he took them and hid them from his brothers.

(Jasher 7:28)
And when Ham begot his firstborn Cush, he gave him the garments in secret, and they were with Cush many days.

(Jasher 7:29)
And Cush also concealed them from his sons and brothers, and when Cush had begotten Nimrod, he gave him those garments through his love for him, and Nimrod grew up, and when he was twenty years old he put on those garments.

(Genesis 10:9) (Jasher 7:30)
And Nimrod became strong when he put on the garments, and God gave him might and strength, and he was a mighty hunter in the earth, yea, he was a mighty hunter in the field, and he hunted the animals and he built altars, and he offered upon them the animals before the Lord: why it is said, Even as Nimrod the mighty hunter before the Lord.

(Jasher 7:31)
And Nimrod strengthened himself, and he rose up from among his brethren, and he fought the battles of his brethren against all their enemies round about.

(Jasher 7:32)
And the Lord delivered all the enemies of his brethren in his hands, and God prospered him from time to time in his battles, and he reigned upon earth.

(Jasher 7:33)
Therefore, it became current in those days, when a man ushered forth those that he had trained up for battle, he would say to them, Like God did to Nimrod, who was a mighty hunter in the earth, and who succeeded in the battles that prevailed against his brethren, that he delivered them from the hands of their enemies, so may God strengthen us and deliver us this day.

(Jasher 7:34)
And when Nimrod was forty years old, at that time there was a war between his brethren and the children of Japheth, so that they were in the power of their enemies.

(Jasher 7:35)
And Nimrod went forth at that time, and he assembled all the sons of Cush and their families, about four hundred and sixty men, and he hired also from some of his friends and acquaintances about eighty men, and be gave them their hire, and he went with them to battle, and when he was on the road, Nimrod strengthened the hearts of the people that went with him.

(Jasher 7:36)
And he said to them, Do not fear, neither be alarmed, for all our enemies will be delivered into our hands, and you may do with them as you please.

(Jasher 7:37)
And all the men that went were about five hundred, and they fought against their enemies, and they destroyed them, and subdued them, and Nimrod placed standing officers over them in their respective places.

(Jasher 7:38)
And he took some of their children as security, and they were all servants to Nimrod and to his brethren, and Nimrod and all the people that were with him turned homeward.

(Jasher 7:39)
And when Nimrod had joyfully returned from battle, after having conquered his enemies, all his brethren, together with those who knew him before, assembled to make him king over them, and they placed the regal crown upon his head.

(Jasher 7:40)
And he set over his subjects and people, princes, judges, and rulers, as is the custom among kings.

(Jasher 7:41)
And he placed Terah the son of Nahor the prince of his host, and he dignified him and elevated him above all his princes.

(Jasher 7:42)
And whilst he was reigning according to his heart's desire, after having conquered all his enemies around, he advised with his counselors to build a city for his palace, and they did so.

(Jasher 7:43)
And they found a large valley opposite to the east, and they built him a large and extensive city, and Nimrod called

the name of the city that he built Shinar, for the Lord had vehemently shaken his enemies and destroyed them.

(Genesis 10:10)
And the beginning of his kingdom was Babel, and Erech, and Accad, and Calneh, in the land of Shinar.

(Genesis 10:11)
Out of that land went forth Asshur, and built Nineveh, and the city Rehoboth, and Calah,

(Genesis 10:12)
And Resen between Nineveh and Calah: the same is a great city.

(Genesis 10:13) (Jasher 7:11...)
And Mizraim begot Ludim, and Anamim, and Lehabim, and Naphtuhim,

(Genesis 10:14) (...Jasher 7:11)
And Pathrusim, and Casluhim, out of whom came Philistim, and Caphtorim.

(Jasher 7:12)
And the sons of Phut were Gebul, Hadan, Benah and Adan.

(Genesis 10:15) (Jasher 7:13...)
And Canaan begot Sidon his firstborn, and Heth,

(Genesis 10:16) (...Jasher 7:13...)
And the Jebusite, and the Amorite, and the Girgasite,

(Genesis 10:17) (...Jasher 7:13...)

And the Hivite, and the Arkite, and the Sinite,

(Genesis 10:18) (...Jasher 7:13)

And the Arvadite, and the Zemarite, and the Hamathite: and afterward were the families of the Canaanites spread abroad.

(Genesis 10:19)

And the border of the Canaanites was from Sidon, as you come to Gerar, to Gaza; as you go, to Sodom, and Gomorrah, and Admah, and Zeboim, even to Lasha.

(Genesis 10:20) (Jasher 7:14)

These are the sons of Ham, after their families, after their tongues, in their countries, and in their nations; and their numbers in those days were about seven hundred and thirty men.

(Genesis 10:21)

To Shem also, the father of all the children of Eber, the brother of Japheth the elder, even to him were children born.

(Genesis 10:22) (Jasher 7:15...)

The children of Shem; Elam, and Asshur, and Arphaxad, and Lud, and Aram, five sons.

(...Jasher 7:15)

And the sons of Elam were Shushan, Machul and Harmon.

(Jasher 7:16)

And the sons of Ashar were Mirus and Mokil, and the sons of Arpachshad were Shelach, Anar and Ashcol.

(Jasher 7:17...)
And the sons of Lud were Pethor and Bizayon.

(Genesis 10:23) (...Jasher 7:17)
And the children of Aram; Uz, and Hul, and Gether, and Mash.

(Jasher 7:18)
These are the sons of Shem, according to their families; and their numbers in those days were about three hundred men.

(Genesis 10:24...) (Jasher 7:19...)
These are the generations of Shem; Shem begot Arpachshad,

(Jubilees 8:1)
In the twenty-ninth jubilee, in the first week, in the beginning thereof Arpachshad took to himself a wife and her name was Rasueja, the daughter of Susan, the daughter of Elam, and she bare him a son in the third year in this week, and he called his name Kainam.

(Jubilees 8:2)
And the son grew, and his father taught him writing, and he went to seek for himself a place where he might seize for himself a city.

(Jubilees 8:3)
And he found a writing which former generations had carved on the rock, and he read what was thereon, and he transcribed it and sinned owing to it; for it contained the teaching of the Watchers in accordance with which they used to observe the omens of the sun and moon and stars in all the signs of heaven.

(Jubilees 8:4)
And he wrote it down and said nothing regarding it; for he

was afraid to speak to Noah about it lest he should be angry with him on account of it.

(...Genesis 10:24...) (...Jasher 7:19...) (Jubilees 8:5)
And in the thirtieth jubilee, in the second week, in the first year thereof, he took to himself a wife, and her name was Melka, the daughter of Madai, the son of Japheth, and in the fourth year and Arphaxad begot a son, and called his name Salah; for he said: Truly I have been sent.

(Jubilees 8:6)
And in the fourth year he was born, and Shelah grew up and took to himself a wife, and her name was Muak, the daughter of Kesed, his father's brother, in the one and thirtieth jubilee, in the fifth week, in the first year thereof.

(...Genesis 10:24) (...Jasher 7:19...) (Jubilees 8:7)
And she bare him a son in the fifth year thereof, and Salah begot Eber; and he called his name Eber: and he took to himself a wife, and her name was Azûrâd, the daughter of Nebrod, in the thirty-second jubilee, in the seventh week, in the third year thereof.

(Genesis 10:25...) (...Jasher 7:19) (Jubilees 8:8)
And to Eber were born two sons. In the sixth year thereof, she bare him a son, and he called the name of the one Peleg; for in his days the sons of men were divided, the children of Noah began to divide the earth among themselves: for this reason he called his name Peleg. And in the latter days, the earth was divided; and the name of the second, his brother, was Joktan meaning that in his day the lives of the sons of men were diminished and lessened.

(Genesis 10:26) (Jasher 7:21...)
And Joktan begot Almodad, and Sheleph, and Hazarmaveth, and Jerah,

(Genesis 10:27) (...Jasher 7:21...)
And Hadoram, and Uzal, and Diklah,

(Genesis 10:28) (...Jasher 7:21...)
And Obal, and Abimael, and Sheba,

(Genesis 10:29) (...Jasher 7:21)
And Ophir, and Havilah, and Jobab: all these were the sons of Joktan.

(Jasher 7:22...)
And Peleg his brother begot Yen, and Yen begot Serug.

(Genesis 10:30)
And their dwelling was from Mesha, as you go to Sephar, a mountain of the east.

(Genesis 10:31)
These are the sons of Shem, after their families, after their tongues, in their lands, after their nations.

(Genesis 10:32)
These are the families of the sons of Noah, after their generations, in their nations: and by these were the nations divided in the earth after the flood.

(Jubilees 8:9)
They divided the earth secretly among themselves, and told it to Noah.

(Jubilees 8:10)
And it came to pass in the beginning of the thirty-third jubilee, that they divided the earth into three parts, for Shem and Ham and Japheth, according to the inheritance of each, in the first year in the first week, when one of us who had been sent, was with them.

(Jubilees 8:11)
And he called his sons, and they drew nigh to him, they and their children, and he divided the earth into the lots, which his three sons were to take in possession, and they reached forth their hands, and took the writing out of the bosom of Noah, their father.

(Jubilees 8:12)
And there came forth on the writing as Shem's lot the middle of the earth which he should take as an inheritance for himself and for his sons for the generations of eternity, from the middle of the mountain range of Rafa, from the mouth of the water from the river Tina, and his portion goes towards the west through the midst of this river, and it extends till it reaches the water of the abysses, out of which this river goes forth and pours its waters into the sea Meat, and this river flows into the great sea. And all that is towards the north is Japheth's, and all that is towards the south belongs to Shem.

(Jubilees 8:13)
And it extends till it reaches Karaso: this is in the bosom of the tongue which looks towards the south.

(Jubilees 8:14)
And his portion extends along the great sea, and it extends in a straight line till it reaches the west of the tongue which looks towards the south: for this sea is named the tongue of the Egyptian Sea.

(Jubilees 8:15)
And it turns from here towards the south towards the mouth of the great sea on the shore of its waters, and it extends to the west to Afra, and it extends till it reaches the waters of the river Gihon, and to the south of the waters of Gihon, to the banks of this river.

(Jubilees 8:16)
And it extends towards the east, till it reaches the Garden of Eden, to the south thereof, to the south and from the east of the whole land of Eden and of the whole east, it turns to the east and proceeds till it reaches the east of the mountain named Rafa, and it descends to the bank of the mouth of the river Tina.

(Jubilees 8:17)
This portion came forth by lot for Shem and his sons, that they should possess it forever to his generations forevermore.

(Jubilees 8:18)
And Noah rejoiced that this portion came forth for Shem and for his sons, and he remembered all that he had spoken with his mouth in prophecy; for he had said: Blessed be the Lord God of Shem And may the Lord dwell in the dwelling of Shem.

(Jubilees 8:19)
And he knew that the Garden of Eden is the holy of holies, and the dwelling of the Lord, and Mount Sinai the center of the desert, and Mount Zion - the center of the navel of the earth: these three were created as holy places facing each other.

(Jubilees 8:20)
And he blessed the God of gods, who had put the word of the Lord into his mouth, and the Lord forevermore.

(Jubilees 8:21)
And he knew that a blessed portion and a blessing had come to Shem and his sons to the generations forever -the whole land of Eden and the whole land of the Red Sea, and the whole land of the east and India, and on the Red Sea and the mountains thereof, and all the land of Bashan, and all the land of Lebanon and the islands of Kaftur, and all the mountains of Sanir and Amana, and the mountains of Asshur in the north, and all the land of Elam, Asshur, and Babel, and Susan and Maedai, and all the mountains of Ararat, and all the region beyond the sea, which is beyond the mountains of Asshur towards the north, a blessed and spacious land, and all that is in it is very good.

(Jubilees 8:22)
And for Ham came forth the second portion, beyond the Gihon towards the south to the right of the Garden, and it extends towards the south and it extends to all the mountains of fire, and it extends towards the west to the sea of Atel and it extends towards the west till it reaches the sea of Mauk - that into which everything which is not destroyed descends.

(Jubilees 8:23)
And it goes forth towards the north to the limits of Gadir, and it goes forth to the coast of the waters of the sea to the waters of the great sea till it draws near to the river Gihon, and goes along the river Gihon till it reaches the right of the Garden of Eden.

(Jubilees 8:24)
And this is the land which came forth for Ham as the portion which he was to occupy forever for himself and his sons to their generations forever.

(Jubilees 8:25)
And for Japheth came forth the third portion beyond the river

Tina to the north of the outflow of its waters, and it extends north - easterly to the whole region of Gog, and to all the country east thereof.

(Jubilees 8:26)
And it extends northerly to the north, and it extends to the mountains of Qelt towards the north, and towards the sea of Mauk, and it goes forth to the east of Gadir as far as the region of the waters of the sea.

(Jubilees 8:27)
And it extends until it approaches the west of Fara and it returns towards Aferag, and it extends easterly to the waters of the sea of Meat.

(Jubilees 8:28)
And it extends to the region of the river Tina in a north-easterly direction until it approaches the boundary of its waters towards the mountain Rafa, and it turns around towards the north.

(Jubilees 8:29)
This is the land which came forth for Japheth and his sons as the portion of his inheritance which he should possess for himself and his sons, for their generations forever; five great islands, and a great land in the north.

(Jubilees 8:30)
But it is cold, and the land of Ham is hot, and the land of Shem is neither hot nor cold, but it is of blended cold and heat.

~ ~ ~

(Jubilees 9:1)
And Ham divided among his sons, and the first portion came forth for Cush towards the east, and to the west of him for Mizraim, and to the west of him for Put, and to the west of him and to the west thereof on the sea for Canaan.

(Jubilees 9:2)
And Shem also divided among his sons, and the first portion came forth for Ham and his sons, to the east of the river Tigris till it approaches the east, the whole land of India, and on the Red Sea on its coast, and the waters of Dedan, and all the mountains of Mebri and Ela, and all the land of Susan and all that is on the side of Pharnak to the Red Sea and the river Tina.

(Jubilees 9:3)
And for Asshur came forth the second Portion, all the land of Asshur and Nineveh and Shinar and to the border of India, and it ascends and skirts the river.

(Jubilees 9:4)
And for Arpachshad came forth the third portion, all the land of the region of the Chaldees to the east of the Euphrates, bordering on the Red Sea, and all the waters of the desert close to the tongue of the sea which looks towards Egypt, all the land of Lebanon and Sanir and Amana to the border of the Euphrates.

(Jubilees 9:5)
And for Aram there came forth the fourth portion, all the land of Mesopotamia between the Tigris and the Euphrates to the north of the Chaldees to the border of the mountains of Asshur and the land of Arara.

(Jubilees 9:6)
And there came forth for Lud the fifth portion, the mountains of Asshur and all appertaining to them till it reaches the Great Sea, and till it reaches the east of Asshur his brother.

(Jubilees 9:7)
And Japheth also divided the land of his inheritance among his sons.

(Jubilees 9:8)
And the first portion came forth for Gomer to the east from the north side to the river Tina; and in the north there came forth for Magog all the inner portions of the north until it reaches to the sea of Meat.

(Jubilees 9:9)
And for Madai came forth as his portion that he should posses from the west of his two brothers to the islands, and to the coasts of the islands.

(Jubilees 9:10)
And for Javan came forth the fourth portion every island and the islands which are towards the border of Lud.

(Jubilees 9:11)
And for Tubal there came forth the fifth portion in the midst of the tongue which approaches towards the border of the portion of Lud to the second tongue, to the region beyond the second tongue to the third tongue.

(Jubilees 9:12)
And for Meshech came forth the sixth portion, all the region beyond the third tongue till it approaches the east of Gadir.

(Jubilees 9:13)
And for Tiras there came forth the seventh portion, four great islands in the midst of the sea, which reach to the portion of Ham and the islands of Kamaturi came out by lot for the sons of Arpachshad as his inheritance.

(Jubilees 9:14)
And thus the sons of Noah divided to their sons in the presence of Noah their father, and he bound them all by an oath, imprecating a curse on everyone that sought to seize the portion which had not fallen to him by his lot.

(Jubilees 9:15)
And they all said, So be it; so be it for themselves and their sons forever throughout their generations till the day of judgment, on which the Lord God shall judge them with a sword and with fire for all the unclean wickedness of their errors, wherewith they have filled the earth with transgression and uncleanness and fornication and sin.

Genesis: Chapter Eleven

(Genesis 11:1)
And the whole earth was of one language, and of one speech.

(Genesis 11:2)
And it came to pass, as they journeyed from the east, that they found a plain in the land of Shinar; and they dwelt there.

(Jasher 7:44)
And Nimrod dwelt in Shinar, and he reigned securely, and he fought with his enemies and he subdued them, and he prospered in all his battles, and his kingdom became very great.

(Jasher 7:45)
And all nations and tongues heard of his fame, and they gathered themselves to him, and they bowed down to the earth, and they brought him offerings, and he became their Lord and king, and they all dwelt with him in the city at Shinar, and Nimrod reigned in the earth over all the sons of Noah, and they were all under his power and counsel.

(Jasher 7:46)
And all the earth was of one tongue and words of union, but Nimrod did not go in the ways of the Lord, and he was more wicked than all the men that were before him, from the days of the flood until those days.

(Jasher 7:47)
And he made gods of wood and stone, and he bowed down

to them, and he rebelled against the Lord, and taught all his subjects and the people of the earth his wicked ways; and Mardon his son was more wicked than his father.

(Jasher 7:48)
And every one that heard of the acts of Mardon the son of Nimrod would say, concerning him, From the wicked goes forth wickedness; therefore, it became a proverb in the whole earth, saying, From the wicked goes forth wickedness, and it was current in the words of men from that time to this.

(Jasher 7:49)
And Terah the son of Nahor, prince of Nimrod's host, was in those days very great in the sight of the king and his subjects, and the king and princes loved him, and they elevated him very high.

(Jasher 7:50) (Jubilees 11:13)
And in this thirty-ninth jubilee, in the second week in the first year, Terah took a wife and her name was Amthelo the daughter of Cornebo, the daughter of Abram, the daughter of his father's sister. And in the seventh year of this week; and the wife of Terah conceived and bare him a son in those days and he called his name Abram, by the name of the father of his mother;

(Jubilees 11:14)
For he had died before his daughter had conceived a son.

(Jasher 7:51)
Terah was seventy years old when he begot him, and Terah called the name of his son that was born to him Abram, because the king had raised him in those days, and dignified him above all his princes that were with him.

~ ~ ~

(Jasher 8:1)
And it was in the night that Abram was born, that all the servants of Terah, and all the wise men of Nimrod, and his conjurers came and ate and drank in the house of Terah, and they rejoiced with him on that night.

(Jasher 8:2)
And when all the wise men and conjurers went out from the house of Terah, they lifted up their eyes toward heaven that night to look at the stars, and they saw, and behold one very large star came from the east and ran in the heavens, and he swallowed up the four stars from the four sides of the heavens.

(Jasher 8:3)
And all the wise men of the king and his conjurers were astonished at the sight, and the sages understood this matter, and they knew its import.

(Jasher 8:4)
And they said to each other, This only betokens the child that has been born to Terah this night, who will grow up and be fruitful, and multiply, and possess all the earth, he and his children forever, and he and his seed will slay great kings, and inherit their lands.

(Jasher 8:5)
And the wise men and conjurers went home that night, and in the morning, all these wise men and conjurers rose up early, and assembled in an appointed house.

(Jasher 8:6)
And they spoke and said to each other, Behold the sight that we saw last night is hidden from the king, it has not been made known to him.

(Jasher 8:7)
And should this thing get known to the king in the latter days, he will say to us, Why have you concealed this matter from me, and then we shall all suffer death; therefore, now let us go and tell the king the sight which we saw, and the interpretation thereof, and we shall then remain clear.

(Jasher 8:8)
And they did so, and they all went to the king and bowed down to him to the ground, and they said, May the king live, may the king live.

(Jasher 8:9)
We heard that a son was born to Terah the son of Nahor, the prince of your host, and we last night came to his house, and we ate and drank and rejoiced with him that night.

(Jasher 8:10)
And when your servants went out from the house of Terah, to go to our respective homes to abide there for the night, we lifted up our eyes to heaven, and we saw a great star coming from the east, and the same star ran with great speed, and swallowed up four great stars, from the four sides of the heavens.

(Jasher 8:11)
And your servants were astonished at the sight which we saw, and were greatly terrified, and we made our judgment upon the sight, and knew by our wisdom the proper interpretation

thereof, that this thing applies to the child that is born to Terah, who will grow up and multiply greatly, and become powerful, and kill all the kings of the earth, and inherit all their lands, he and his seed forever.

(Jasher 8:12)
And now our Lord and king, behold we have truly acquainted you with what we have seen concerning this child.

(Jasher 8:13)
If it seems good to the king to give his father value for this child, we will slay him before he shall grow up and increase in the land, and his evil increase against us, that we and our children perish through his evil.

(Jasher 8:14)
And the king heard their words and they seemed good in his sight, and he sent and called for Terah, and Terah came before the king.

(Jasher 8:15)
And the king said to Terah, I have been told that a son was last night born to you, and after this manner was observed in the heavens at his birth.

(Jasher 8:16)
And now therefore give me the child, that we may slay him before his evil springs up against us, and I will give you for his value, your house full of silver and gold.

(Jasher 8:17)
And Terah answered the king and said to him: My Lord and king, I have heard your words, and your servant shall do all that his king desires.

(Jasher 8:18)
But my Lord and king, I will tell you what happened to me last night, that I may see what advice the king will give his servant, and then I will answer the king upon what he has just spoken; and the king said, Speak.

(Jasher 8:19)
And Terah said to the king, Ayon, son of Mored, came to me last night, saying,

(Jasher 8:20)
Give to me the great and beautiful horse that the king gave you, and I will give you silver and gold, and straw and provender for its value; and I said to him, Wait till I see the king concerning your words, and behold whatever the king says, that will I do.

(Jasher 8:21)
And now my Lord and king, behold I have made this thing known to you, and the advice which my king will give to his servant, that will I follow.

(Jasher 8:22)
And the king heard the words of Terah, and his anger was kindled and he considered him in the light of a fool.

(Jasher 8:23)
And the king answered Terah, and he said to him, Are you so silly, ignorant, or deficient in understanding, to do this thing, to give your beautiful horse for silver and gold or even for straw and provender?

(Jasher 8:24)
Are you so short of silver and gold, that you should do this

thing, because you cannot obtain straw and provender to feed your horse? And what is silver and gold to you, or straw and provender, that you should give away that fine horse which I gave you, like which there is none to be had on the whole earth?

(Jasher 8:25)
And the king left off speaking, and Terah answered the king, saying, Like to this has the king spoken to his servant;

(Jasher 8:26)
I beseech you, my Lord and king, what is this which you said to me, saying, Give your son that we may slay him, and I will give you silver and gold for his value; what shall I do with silver and gold after the death of my son? Who shall inherit me? Surely then at my death, the silver and gold will return to my king who gave it.

(Jasher 8:27)
And when the king heard the words of Terah, and the parable which he brought concerning the king, it grieved him greatly and he was vexed at this thing, and his anger burned within him.

(Jasher 8:28)
And Terah saw that the anger of the king was kindled against him, and he answered the king, saying, All that I have is in the king's power; whatever the king desires to do to his servant, that let him do, yea, even my son, he is in the king's power, without value in exchange, he and his two brothers that are older than he.

(Jasher 8:29)
And the king said to Terah, No, but I will purchase your

younger son for a price.

(Jasher:30)
And Terah answered the king, saying, I beseech you my Lord and king to let your servant speak a word before you, and let the king hear the word of his servant, and Terah said, Let my king give me three days time till I consider this matter within myself, and consult with my family concerning the words of my king; and he pressed the king greatly to agree to this.

(Jasher 8:31)
And the king hearkened to Terah, and he did so and he gave him three days time, and Terah went out from the king's presence, and he came home to his family and spoke to them all the words of the king; and the people were greatly afraid.

(Jasher 8:32)
And it was in the third day that the king sent to Terah, saying, Send me your son for a price as I spoke to you; and should you not do this, I will send and slay all you have in your house, so that you shall not even have a dog remaining.

(Jasher 8:33)
And Terah hastened, as the thing was urgent from the king, and he took a child from one of his servants, which his handmaid had born to him that day, and Terah brought the child to the king and received value for him.

(Jasher 8:34)
And the Lord was with Terah in this matter, that Nimrod might not cause Abram's death, and the king took the child from Terah and with all his might dashed his head to the ground, for he thought it had been Abram; and this was concealed from him from that day, and it was forgotten by the king, as it

was the will of Providence not to suffer Abram's death.

(Jasher 8:35)
And Terah took Abram his son secretly, together with his mother and nurse, and he concealed them in a cave, and he brought them their provisions monthly.

(Jasher 8:36)
And the Lord was with Abram in the cave and he grew up, and Abram was in the cave ten years, and the king and his princes, soothsayers and sages, thought that the king had killed Abram.

~ ~ ~

(Jasher 9:1)
And Haran, the son of Terah, Abram's oldest brother, took a wife in those days.

(Jasher 9:2)
Haran was thirty-nine years old when he took her; and the wife of Haran conceived and bare a son, and he called his name Lot.

(Jasher 9:3)
And she conceived again and bare a daughter, and she called her name Milca; and she again conceived and bare a daughter, and she called her name Sarai.

(Jasher 9:4)
Haran was forty-two years old when he begot Sarai, which

was in the tenth year of the life of Abram; and in those days Abram and his mother and nurse went out from the cave, as the king and his subjects had forgotten the affair of Abram.

(Jasher 9:5)
And when Abram came out from the cave, he went to Noah and his son Shem, and he remained with them to learn the instruction of the Lord and his ways, and no man knew where Abram was, and Abram served Noah and Shem his son for a long time.

(Jasher 9:6)
And Abram was in Noah's house thirty-nine years, and Abram knew the Lord from three years old, and he went in the ways of the Lord until the day of his death, as Noah and his son Shem had taught him; and all the sons of the earth in those days greatly transgressed against the Lord, and they rebelled against him and they served other gods, and they forgot the Lord who had created them in the earth; and the inhabitants of the earth made to themselves, at that time, every man his God; gods of wood and stone which could neither speak, hear, nor deliver, and the sons of men served them and they became their gods.

(Jasher 9:7)
And the king and all his servants, and Terah with all his household were then the first of those that served gods of wood and stone.

(Jasher 9:8)
And Terah had twelve gods of large size, made of wood and stone, after the twelve months of the year, and he served each one monthly, and every month Terah would bring his meat

offering and drink offering to his gods; thus did Terah all the days.

(Jasher 9:9)
And all that generation were wicked in the sight of the Lord, and they thus made every man his God, but they forsook the Lord who had created them.

(Jasher 9:10)
And there was not a man found in those days in the whole earth, who knew the Lord (for they served each man his own god) except Noah and his household, and all those who were under his counsel knew the Lord in those days.

(Jasher 9:11)
And Abram the son of Terah was waxing great in those days in the house of Noah, and no man knew it, and the Lord was with him.

(Jasher 9:12)
And the Lord gave Abram an understanding heart, and he knew all the works of that generation were vain, and that all their gods were vain and were of no avail.

(Jasher 9:13)
And Abram saw the sun shining upon the earth, and Abram said to himself Surely now this sun that shines upon the earth is God, and him will I serve.

(Jasher 9:14)
And Abram served the sun in that day and he prayed to him, and when evening came the sun set as usual, and Abram said within himself, Surely this cannot be God?

(Jasher 9:15)
And Abram still continued to speak within himself, Who is he who made the heavens and the earth? Who created upon earth? Where is he?

(Jasher 9:16)
And night darkened over him, and he lifted up his eyes toward the west, north, south, and east, and he saw that the sun had vanished from the earth, and the day became dark.

(Jasher 9:17)
And Abram saw the stars and moon before him, and he said, Surely, this is the God Who created the whole earth as well as man, and behold these his servants are gods around him: and Abram served the moon and prayed to it all that night.

(Jasher 9:18)
And in the morning when it was light and the sun shone upon the earth as usual, Abram saw all the things that the Lord God had made upon earth.

(Jasher 9:19)
And Abram said to himself Surely these are not gods that made the earth and all mankind, but these are the servants of God, and Abram remained in the house of Noah and there knew the Lord and his ways and he served the Lord all the days of his life, and all that generation forgot the Lord, and served other gods of wood and stone, and rebelled all their days.

(Jasher 9:20)
And king Nimrod reigned securely, and all the earth was under his control, and all the earth was of one tongue and words of union.

(Genesis 11:3) (Jasher 9:21...) (...Jubilees 10:20)

And all the princes of Nimrod and his great men took counsel together; Phut, Mitzraim, Cush and Canaan with their families, and they said one to another, Come, let us make brick, and burn them throughly. And they had brick for stone, and slime had they for mortar - the clay with which they cemented them together was asphalt which comes out of the sea, and out of the fountains of water in the land of Shinar.

(Genesis 11:4) (...Jasher 9:21)

And they said, Come, let us build us a city and a strong tower, whose top may reach to heaven; and let us make us a name, so that we may reign upon the whole world, in order that the evil of our enemies may cease from us, that we may reign mightily over them, lest we be scattered abroad on the face of the whole earth on account of their wars.

(Jasher 9:22)

And they all went before the king, and they told the king these words, and the king agreed with them in this affair, and he did so.

(Jasher 9:23)

And all the families assembled consisting of about six hundred thousand men, and they went to seek an extensive piece of ground to build the city and the tower, and they sought in the whole earth and they found none like one valley at the east of the land of Shinar, about two days walk, and they journeyed there and they dwelt there.

~ ~ ~

(Jubilees 10:18)
And in the three and thirtieth jubilee, in the first year in the second week, Peleg took to himself a wife, whose name was Lomna the daughter of Sinaar, and she bare him a son in the fourth year of this week, and he called his name Reu; for he said: Behold the children of men have become evil through the wicked purpose of building for themselves a city and a tower in the land of Shinar.

(Jubilees 10:19)
For they departed from the land of Ararat eastward to Shinar; for in his days they built the city and the tower, saying, Go to, let us ascend thereby into heaven.

~ ~ ~

(Jasher 9:24) (Jubilees 10:20...)
And they began to build, and in the fourth week they made bricks with burn fires to build the city and the tower that they had imagined to complete.

(Jasher 9:25)
And the building of the tower was to them a transgression and a sin, and they began to build it, and whilst they were building against the Lord God of heaven, they imagined in their hearts to war against him and to ascend into heaven.

(Jasher 9:26)
And all these people and all the families divided themselves in three parts; the first said We will ascend into heaven and fight against him; the second said, We will ascend to heaven and place our own gods there and serve them; and the third

part said, We will ascend to heaven and smite him with bows and spears; and God knew all their works and all their evil thoughts, and he saw the city and the tower which they were building.

(Jasher 9:27)
And when they were building they built themselves a great city and a very high and strong tower; and on account of its height the mortar and bricks did not reach the builders in their ascent to it, until those who went up had completed a full year, and after that, they reached to the builders and gave them the mortar and the bricks; thus was it done daily.

(Jasher 9:28)
And behold these ascended and others descended the whole day; and if a brick should fall from their hands and get broken, they would all weep over it, and if a man fell and died, none of them would look at him.

(Jasher 9:29)
And the Lord knew their thoughts, and it came to pass when they were building they cast the arrows toward the heavens, and all the arrows fell upon them filled with blood, and when they saw them they said to each other, Surely we have slain all those that are in heaven.

(Jasher 9:30)
For this was from the Lord in order to cause them to err, and in order; to destroy them from off the face of the ground.

(Jasher 9:31) (Jubilees 10:21)
And they built the tower and the city, and they did this thing daily until many days and years were elapsed - forty-three years, they were building it; its breadth was 203 bricks, and

the height of a brick was the third of one; its height amounted to 5433 cubits and 2 palms, and the extent of one wall was thirteen stades.

(Genesis 11:5)

And the Lord came down to see the city and the tower, which the children of men built.

(Genesis 11:6) (Jubilees 10:22...)

And the Lord said to us: Behold, the people is one, and they have all one language; and this they begin to do: and now nothing will be restrained from them, which they have imagined to do.

(Genesis 11:7) (Jasher 9:32) (...Jubilees 10:22)

And God said to the seventy angels who stood foremost before him, to those who were near to him, saying, Come, let us go down, and confuse their tongues, that one man shall not understand the language, that they may not understand one another's speech and they may be dispersed into cities and nations, and one purpose will no longer abide with them till the day of judgment. And they did so to them.

(Jubilees 10:23)
And the Lord descended, and we descended with him to see the city and the tower which the children of men had built.

(Jasher 9:33) (Jubilees 10:24...)
And he confounded their language, and from that day following, they forgot each man his neighbor's tongue, and they could not understand to speak in one tongue, and when the builder took from the hands of his neighbor lime or stone which he did not order, the builder would cast it away and throw it upon his neighbor, that he would die.

(Jasher 9:34)
And they did so many days, and they killed many of them in this manner.

(Jasher 9:35)
And the Lord smote the three divisions that were there, and he punished them according to their works and designs; those who said, We will ascend to heaven and serve our gods, became like apes and elephants; and those who said, We will smite the heaven with arrows, the Lord killed them, one man through the hand of his neighbor; and the third division of those who said, We will ascend to heaven and fight against him, the Lord scattered them throughout the earth.

(Genesis 11:8) (Jasher 9:36, 37...) (...Jubilees 10:24)
And those who were left among them, when they knew and understood the evil which was coming upon them, they forsook the building. So the Lord scattered them abroad from there on the face of all the earth: and they left off to build the city and the tower.

(Genesis 11:9) (...Jasher 9:37) (Jubilees 10:25)
For this reason, He called that place, the whole land of Shinar, Babel. Behold it was at the east of the land of Shinar. Therefore, the name of it called Babel; because there, the Lord confounded the language of all the children of men of the earth: and from there they were dispersed into their cities, each according to his language and his nation - the Lord scattered them abroad on the face of all the earth.

(Jubilees 10:26)
And the Lord sent a mighty wind against the tower and overthrew it on the earth, and behold it was between Asshur and Babylon in the land of Shinar, and they called its name Overthrow.

(Jasher 9:38)
And as to the tower which the sons of men built, the earth opened its mouth and swallowed up one third part thereof, and a fire also descended from heaven and burned another third, and the other third is left to this day, and it is of that part which was aloft, and its circumference is three days walk.

(Jasher 9:39)
And many of the sons of men died in that tower, a people without number.

~ ~ ~

(Jasher 10:1)
And Peleg the son of Eber died in those days, in the forty-eighth year of the life of Abram son of Terah, and all the days of Peleg were two hundred and thirty-nine years.

(Jasher 10:2)
And when the Lord had scattered the sons of men on account of their sin at the tower, behold they spread forth into many divisions, and all the sons of men were dispersed into the four corners of the earth.

(Jubilees 10:27)
In the fourth week, in the first year ,in the beginning thereof, in the four and thirtieth jubilee, were they dispersed from the land of Shinar.

(Jasher 10:3)
And all the families became each according to its language, its land, or its city.

(Jasher 10:4)
And the sons of men built many cities according to their families, in all the places where they went, and throughout the earth where the Lord had scattered them.

(Jasher 10:5)
And some of them built cities in places from which they were afterward extirpated, and they called these cities after their own names, or the names of their children, or after their particular occurrences.

(Jubilees 10:35)
And Japheth and his sons went towards the sea and dwelt in the land of their portion, and Madai saw the land of the sea and it did not please him, and he begged a portion from Ham and Asshur and Arpachshad, his wife's brother, and he dwelt in the land of Media, near to his wife's brother until this day.

(Jubilees 10:36)
And he called his dwelling-place, and the dwelling-place of his sons, Media, after the name of their father Madai.

(Jasher 10:6)
And the sons of Japheth the son of Noah went and built themselves cities in the places where they were scattered, and they called all their cities after their names, and the sons of Japheth were divided upon the face of the earth into many divisions and languages.

(Jasher 10:7)
And these are the sons of Japheth according to their families, Gomer, Magog, Medai, Javan, Tubal, Meshech and Tiras; these are the children of Japheth according to their generations.

(Jasher 10:8)
And the children of Gomer, according to their cities, were the Francum, who dwell in the land of Franza, by the river Franza, by the river Senah.

(Jasher 10:9)
And the children of Rephath are the Bartonim, who dwell in the land of Bartonia by the river Ledah, which empties its waters in the great sea Gihon, that is, oceanus.

(Jasher 10:10)
And the children of Tugarma are ten families, and these are their names: Buzar, Parzunac, Balgar, Elicanum, Ragbib, Tarki, Bid, Zebuc, Ongal and Tilmaz; all these spread and rested in the north and built themselves cities.

(Jasher 10:11)
And they called their cities after their own names, those are they who abide by the rivers Hithlah and Italac to this day.

(Jasher 10:12)
But the families of Angoli, Balgar and Parzunac, they dwell by the great river Dubnee; and the names of their cities are also according to their own names.

(Jasher 10:13)
And the children of Javan are the Javanim who dwell in the land of Makdonia, and the children of Medaiare are the Orelum that dwell in the land of Curson, and the children of Tubal are those that dwell in the land of Tuskanah by the river Pashiah.

(Jasher 10:14)
And the children of Meshech are the Shibashni and the

children of Tiras are Rushash, Cushni, and Ongolis; all these went and built themselves cities; those are the cities that are situate by the sea Jabus by the river Cura, which empties itself in the river Tragan.

(Jasher 10:15)
And the children of Elishah are the Almanim, and they also went and built themselves cities; those are the cities situate between the mountains of Job and Shibathmo; and of them were the people of Lumbardi who dwell opposite the mountains of Job and Shibathmo, and they conquered the land of Italia and remained there to this day.

(Jasher 10:16)
And the children of Chittim are the Romim who dwell in the valley of Canopia by the river Tibreu.

(Jasher 10:17)
And the children of Dudonim are those who dwell in the cities of the sea Gihon, in the land of Bordna.

(Jasher 10:18)
These are the families of the children of Japheth according to their cities and languages, when they were scattered after the tower, and they called their cities after their names and occurrences; and these are the names of all their cities according to their families, which they built in those days after the tower.

(Jasher 10:19)
And the children of Ham were Cush, Mitzraim, Phut and Canaan according to their generation and cities.

(Jubilees 10:28)
And Ham and his sons went into the land which he was to occupy, which he acquired as his portion in the land of the south.

(Jasher 10:20)
All these went and built themselves cities as they found fit places for them, and they called their cities after the names of their fathers Cush, Mitzraim, Phut and Canaan.

(Jasher 10:21)
And the children of Mitzraim are the Ludim, Anamim, Lehabim, Naphtuchim, Pathrusim, Casluchim and Caphturim, seven families.

(Jasher 10:22)
All these dwell by the river Sihor, that is the brook of Egypt, and they built themselves cities and called them after their own names.

(Jasher 10:23)
And the children of Pathros and Casloch intermarried together, and from them went forth the Pelishtim, the Azathim, and the Gerarim, the Githim and the Ekronim, in all five families; these also built themselves cities, and they called their cities after the names of their fathers to this day.

(Jasher 10:24)
And the children of Canaan also built themselves cities, and they called their cities after their names, eleven cities and others without number.

(Jasher 10:25)
And four men from the family of Ham went to the land of the

plain; these are the names of the four men, Sodom, Gomorrah, Admah and Zeboyim.

(Jasher 10:26)
And these men built themselves four cities in the land of the plain, and they called the names of their cities after their own names.

(Jasher 10:27)
And they and their children and all belonging to them dwelt in those cities, and they were fruitful and multiplied greatly and dwelt peaceably.

(Jasher 10:28)
And Seir the son of Hur, son of Hivi, son of Canaan, went and found a valley opposite to Mount Paran, and he built a city there, and he and his seven sons and his household dwelt there, and he called the city which he built Seir, according to his name; that is the land of Seir to this day.

~ ~ ~

(Jubilees 10:29)
And Canaan saw the land of Lebanon to the river of Egypt, that it was very good, and he did not go into the land of his inheritance to the west, that is to the sea, instead he dwelt in the land of Lebanon, eastward and westward from the border of Jordan and from the border of the sea.

(Jubilees 10:30)
And Ham, his father, and Cush and Mizraim his brothers said to him: You have settled in a land which is not yours, and

which did not fall to us by lot: do not do so; for if you do so, you and your sons will fall in the land and be accursed through sedition; for by sedition you have settled, and by sedition will your children fall, and you shall be rooted out forever.

(Jubilees 10:31)
Do not dwell in the dwelling of Shem; for to Shem and to his sons did it come by their lot.

(Jubilees 10:32)
Cursed are you, and cursed shall you be beyond all the sons of Noah, by the curse by which we bound ourselves by an oath in the presence of the holy judge, and in the presence of Noah our father.

(Jubilees 10:33)
But he did not harken to them, and dwelt in the land of Lebanon from Hamath to the entering of Egypt, he and his sons until this day. And for this reason, that land is named Canaan.

~ ~ ~

(Jasher 10:29)
These are the families of the children of Ham, according to their languages and cities, when they were scattered to their countries after the tower.

(Jasher 10:30)
And some of the children of Shem son of Noah, father of all the children of Eber, also went and built themselves cities in

the places wherein they were scattered, and they called their cities after their names.

(Jasher 10:31)
And the sons of Shem were Elam, Ashur, Arpachshad, Lud and Aram, and they built themselves cities and called the names of all their cities after their names.

(Jasher 10:32)
And Ashur son of Shem and his children and household went forth at that time, a very large body of them, and they went to a distant land that they found, and they met with a very extensive valley in the land that they went to, and they built themselves four cities, and they called them after their own names and occurrences.

(Jasher 10:33)
And these are the names of the cities which the children of Ashur built, Ninevah, Resen, Calach and Rehobother; and the children of Ashur dwell there to this day.

(Jasher 10:34)
And the children of Aram also went and built themselves a city, and they called the name of the city Uz after their eldest brother, and they dwell therein; that is the land of Uz to this day.

(Jasher 10:35)
And in the second year after the tower a man from the house of Ashur, whose name was Bela, went from the land of Ninevah to sojourn with his household wherever he could find a place; and they came until opposite the cities of the plain against Sodom, and they dwelt there.

(Jasher 10:36)
And the man rose up and built there a small city, and called its name Bela, after his name; that is the land of Zoar to this day.

(Jasher 10:37)
And these are the families of the children of Shem according to their language and cities, after they were scattered upon the earth after the tower.

(Jasher 10:38)
And every kingdom, city, and family of the families of the children of Noah built themselves many cities after this.

(Jasher 10:39)
And they established governments in all their cities, in order to be regulated by their orders; so did all the families of the children of Noah forever.

~ ~ ~

(Jasher 11:1)
And Nimrod son of Cush was still in the land of Shinar, and he reigned over it and dwelt there, and he built cities in the land of Shinar.

(Jasher 11:2)
And these are the names of the four cities which he built, and he called their names after the occurrences that happened to them in the building of the tower.

(Jasher 11:3)
And he called the first Babel, saying, Because the Lord there confounded the language of the whole earth; and the name of the second he called Erech, because from there God dispersed them.

(Jasher 11:4)
And the third he called Eched, saying that there was a great battle at that place; and the fourth he called Calnah, because his princes and mighty men were consumed there, and they vexed the Lord, they rebelled and transgressed against him.

(Jasher 11:5)
And when Nimrod had built these cities in the land of Shinar, he placed in them the remainder of his people, his princes and his mighty men that were left in his kingdom.

(Jasher 11:6)
And Nimrod dwelt in Babel, and he there renewed his reign over the rest of his subjects, and he reigned securely, and the subjects and princes of Nimrod called his name Amraphel, saying that at the tower his princes and men fell through his means.

(Jasher 11:7)
And notwithstanding this, Nimrod did not return to the Lord, and he continued in wickedness and teaching wickedness to the sons of men; and Mardon, his son, was worse than his father, and continued to add to the abominations of his father.

(Jasher 11:8)
And he caused the sons of men to sin, therefore it is said, From the wicked goes forth wickedness.

(Jasher 11:9)
At that time there was war between the families of the children of Ham, as they were dwelling in the cities which they had built.

(Jasher 11:10)
And Chedorlaomer, king of Elam, went away from the families of the children of Ham, and he fought with them and he subdued them, and he went to the five cities of the plain and he fought against them and he subdued them, and they were under his control.

(Jasher 11:11)
And they served him twelve years, and they gave him a yearly tax.

(Jasher 11:12)
At that time Nahor died, son of Serug, in the forty-ninth year of the life of Abram son of Terah.

(Jasher 11:13)
And in the fiftieth year of the life of Abram son of Terah, Abram came forth from the house of Noah, and went to his father's house.

(Genesis 11:10)
These are the generations of Shem: Shem was a hundred years old, and begot Arphaxad two years after the flood:

(Genesis 11:11)
And Shem lived after he begot Arphaxad five hundred years, and begot sons and daughters.

(Genesis 11:12)
And Arphaxad lived five and thirty years, and begot Salah:

(Genesis 11:13)
And Arphaxad lived after he begot Salah four hundred and three years, and begot sons and daughters.

(Genesis 11:14)
And Salah lived thirty years, and begot Eber:

(Genesis 11:15)
And Salah lived after he begot Eber four hundred and three years, and begot sons and daughters.

(Genesis 11:16)
And Eber lived four and thirty years, and begot Peleg:

(Genesis 11:17)
And Eber lived after he begot Peleg four hundred and thirty years, and begot sons and daughters.

(Genesis 11:18)
And Peleg lived thirty years, and begot Reu:

(Genesis 11:19)
And Peleg lived after he begot Reu two hundred and nine years, and begot sons and daughters.

(Genesis 11:20...) (Jubilees 11:1)
And Reu lived two and thirty years, and in the thirty-fifth jubilee, in the third week, in the first year thereof, Reu took to himself a wife, and her name was Ôrâ, the daughter of Ûr, the

son of Kesed, and she bare him a son, and he called his name Sêrôh, in the seventh year of this week in this jubilee.

(Genesis 11:21)

And Reu lived after he begot Serug two hundred and seven years, and begot sons and daughters.

(Jubilees 11:2)
And the sons of Noah began to war on each other, to take captive and to slay each other, and to shed the blood of men on the earth, and to eat blood, and to build strong cities, and walls, and towers, and individuals began to exalt themselves above the nation, and to found the beginnings of kingdoms, and to go to war people against people, and nation against nation, and city against city, and all began to do evil, and to acquire arms, and to teach their sons war, and they began to capture cities, and to sell male and female slaves.

(Jubilees 11:3)
And Ûr, the son of Kesed, built the city of Ara of the Chaldees, and called its name after his own name and the name of his father. And they made for themselves molten images, and they worshipped each the idol, the molten image which they had made for themselves, and they began to make graven images and unclean simulacra, and malignant spirits assisted and seduced them into committing transgression and uncleanness.

(Jubilees 11:4)
And the prince Mastêmâ exerted himself to do all this, and he sent forth other spirits, those which were put under his hand, to do all manner of wrong and sin, and all manner of transgression, to corrupt and destroy, and to shed blood on the earth.

(...Genesis 11:20) (Jubilees 11:5)
For this reason, he called the name of Sêrôh, Serug, for everyone turned to do all manner of sin and transgression.

(Jubilees 11:6)
And he grew up, and dwelt in Ur of the Chaldees, near to the father of his wife's mother, and he worshipped idols, and he took to himself a wife in the thirty-sixth jubilee, in the fifth week, in the first year thereof, and her name was Melka, the daughter of Kaber, the daughter of his father's brother.

(Genesis 11:22) (...Jasher 7:22...) (Jubilees 11:7)
And Serug lived thirty years, and begot Nahor: in the first year of this week, and he grew and dwelt in Ur of the Chaldees, and his father taught him the researches of the Chaldees to divine and augur, according to the signs of heaven.

(Genesis 11:23)
And Serug lived after he begot Nahor two hundred years, and begot sons and daughters.

(Jubilees 11:8)
And in the thirty-seventh jubilee in the sixth week, in the first year thereof, Nahor took to himself a wife, and her name was Ijaska, the daughter of Nestag of the Chaldees.

(Genesis 11:24) (...Jasher 7:22...) (Jubilees 11:9)
And Nahor lived nine and twenty years, and begot Terah: in the seventh year of this week.

(Jubilees 11:10)
And the prince Mastêmâ sent ravens and birds to devour the seed which was sown in the land, in order to destroy the land, and rob the children of men of their labors. Before they could

plough in the seed, the ravens picked it from the surface of the ground.

(Jubilees 11:11)
And for this reason, he called his name Terah because the ravens and the birds reduced them to destitution and devoured their seed.

(Jubilees 11:12)
And the years began to be barren, owing to the birds, and they devoured all the fruit of the trees from the trees: it was only with great effort that they could save a little of all the fruit of the earth in their days.

(Genesis 11:25)

And Nahor lived after he begot Terah a hundred and nineteen years, and begot sons and daughters.

(...Jasher 7:22)
And Terah was thirty-eight years old, and he begot Haran and Nahor.

(Genesis 11:26) (Jasher 7:51)

And Terah lived seventy years, and begot Abram, Nahor, and Haran.

(Genesis 11:27)

Now these are the generations of Terah: Terah begot Abram, Nahor, and Haran; and Haran begot Lot.

(Jasher 11:14)
And Abram knew the Lord, and he went in his ways and instructions, and the Lord his God was with him.

(Jubilees 11:15)
And the child began to understand the errors of the earth that all went astray after graven images and after uncleanness, and his father taught him writing, and he was two weeks of years old, and he separated himself from his father, that he might not worship idols with him.

(Jubilees 11:16)
And he began to pray to the Creator of all things that He might save him from the errors of the children of men, and that his portion should not fall into error after uncleanness and vileness.

(Jubilees 11:17)
And the seed time came for the sowing of seed on the land, and they all went forth together to protect their seed against the ravens, and Abram went forth with those that went, and the child was a lad of fourteen years.

(Jubilees 11:18)
And a cloud of ravens came to devour the seed, and Abram ran to meet them before they settled on the ground, and cried to them before they settled on the ground to devour the seed, and said, Descend not: return to the place where you came. And they proceeded to turn back.

(Jubilees 11:19)
And he caused the clouds of ravens to turn back that day seventy times, and of all the ravens throughout all the land where Abram was there settled there not so much as one.

(Jubilees 11:20)
And all who were with him throughout all the land saw him cry out, and all the ravens turn back, and his name became

great in all the land of the Chaldees.

(Jubilees 11:21)
And there came to him this year all those that wished to sow, and he went with them until the time of sowing ceased: and they sowed their land, and that year they brought enough grain home and eat and were satisfied.

(Jubilees 11:22)
And in the first year of the fifth week, Abram taught those who made implements for oxen, the artificers in wood, and they made a vessel above the ground, facing the frame of the plough, in order to put the seed thereon, and the seed fell down therefrom on the share of the plough, and was hidden in the earth, and they no longer feared the ravens.

(Jubilees 11:23)
And after this manner they made vessels above the ground on all the frames of the ploughs, and they sowed and tilled all the land, according as Abram commanded them, and they no longer feared the birds.

~ ~ ~

(Jubilees 12:1)
And it came to pass in the sixth week, in the seventh year thereof, that Abram said to Terah his father, saying, Father!

(Jubilees 12:2)
And he said, Behold, here am I, my son. And he said, What help and profit have we from those idols which you worship, And before which you bow yourself?

(Jubilees 12:3)
For there is no spirit in them, For they are dumb forms, and a misleading of the heart. Worship them not:

(Jubilees 12:4)
Worship the God of heaven, Who causes the rain and the dew to descend on the earth and does everything on the earth, and has created everything by His word, and all life is from before His face.

(Jubilees 12:5)
Why do you worship things that have no spirit in them? For they are the work of men's hands, and on your shoulders, do you bear them, and you have no help from them, but they are a great cause of shame to those who make them, And a misleading of the heart to those who worship them: Worship them not.

(Jubilees 12:6)
And his father said to him, I also know it, my son, but what shall I do with a people who have made me to serve before them?

(Jubilees 12:7)
And if I tell them the truth, they will slay me; for their soul cleaves to them to worship them and honor them.

(Jubilees 12:8)
Keep silent, my son, lest they slay you. And these words he spoke to his two brothers, and they were angry with him and he kept silent.

(Jasher 11:15)
And Terah his father was in those days, still captain of the

host of king Nimrod, and he still followed strange gods.

(Genesis 11:29) (Jasher 12:44...) (Jubilees 12:9,11)

And at that time, in the fortieth jubilee, in the second week, in the seventh year thereof, Abram and Nahor took them wives: the daughters of their brother Haran; the name of Abram's wife was Sarai, the daughter of his father, and she became his wife; and the name of Nahor's wife, Milcah, the daughter of Haran, the father of Milcah, and the father of Iscah.

(Jubilees 12:10)

And Haran, his brother, took to himself a wife in the third year of the third week, and she bare him a son in the seventh year of this week, and he called his name Lot.

(Genesis 11:30) (...Jasher 12:44)

But Sarai, wife of Abram, was barren; she had no child in those days.

(Jubilees 12:12)

And in the sixtieth year of the life of Abram, that is, in the fourth week, in the fourth year thereof, Abram arose by night, and burned the house of the idols, and he burned all that was in the house and no man knew it.

(Jubilees 12:13)

And they arose in the night and sought to save their gods from the midst of the fire.

(Jubilees 12:13)

And Haran hasted to save them, but the fire flamed over him, and he was burnt in the fire, and he died in Ur of the Chaldees before Terah his father, and they buried him in Ur of the Chaldees.

~ ~ ~

(Jasher 11:16)
And Abram came to his father's house and saw twelve gods standing there in their temples, and the anger of Abram was kindled when he saw these images in his father's house.

(Jasher 11:17)
And Abram said, As the Lord lives these images shall not remain in my father's house; so shall the Lord Who created me do to me if in three days time I do not break them all.

(Jasher 11:18)
And Abram went from them, and his anger burned within him. And Abram hastened and went from the chamber to his father's outer court, and he found his father sitting in the court, and all his servants with him, and Abram came and sat before him.

(Jasher 11:19)
And Abram asked his father, saying, Father, tell me where is God Who created heaven and earth, and all the sons of men upon earth, and Who created you and me. And Terah answered his son Abram and said, Behold those who created us are all with us in the house.

(Jasher 11:20)
And Abram said to his father, My Lord, shew them to me I pray you; and Terah brought Abram into the chamber of the inner court, and Abram saw, and behold the whole room was full of gods of wood and stone, twelve great images and others less than they without number.

(Jasher 11:21)
And Terah said to his son, Behold these are they which made all you see upon earth, and which created me and you, and all mankind.

(Jasher 11:22)
And Terah bowed down to his gods, and he then went away from them, and Abram, his son, went away with him.

(Jasher 11:23)
And when Abram had gone from them he went to his mother and sat before her, and he said to his mother, Behold, my father has shown me those who made heaven and earth, and all the sons of men.

(Jasher 11:24)
Now, therefore, hasten and fetch a kid from the flock, and make of it savory meat, that I may bring it to my father's gods as an offering for them to eat; perhaps I may thereby become acceptable to them.

(Jasher 11:25)
And his mother did so, and she fetched a kid, and made savory meat thereof, and brought it to Abram, and Abram took the savory meat from his mother and brought it before his father's gods, and he drew nigh to them that they might eat; and Terah his father, did not know of it.

(Jasher 11:26)
And Abram saw on the day when he was sitting among them, that they had no voice, no hearing, no motion, and not one of them could stretch forth his hand to eat.

(Jasher 11:27)
And Abram mocked them, and said, Surely the savory meat that I prepared has not pleased them, or perhaps it was too little for them, and for that reason they would not eat; therefore, tomorrow I will prepare fresh savory meat, better and more plentiful than this, in order that I may see the result.

(Jasher 11:28)
And it was on the next day that Abram directed his mother concerning the savory meat, and his mother rose and fetched three fine kids from the flock, and she made of them some excellent savory meat, such as her son was fond of, and she gave it to her son Abram; and Terah his father did not know of it.

(Jasher 11:29)
And Abram took the savory meat from his mother, and brought it before his father's gods into the chamber; and he came nigh to them that they might eat, and he placed it before them, and Abram sat before them all day, thinking perhaps they might eat.

(Jasher 11:30)
And Abram viewed them, and behold they had neither voice nor hearing, nor did one of them stretch forth his hand to the meat to eat.

(Jasher 11:31)
And in the evening of that day in that house Abram was clothed with the spirit of God.

(Jasher 11:32)
And he called out and said, Woe to my father and this wicked generation, whose hearts are all inclined to vanity, who

serve these idols of wood and stone which can neither eat, smell, hear nor speak, who have mouths without speech, eyes without sight, ears without hearing, hands without feeling, and legs which cannot move; like them are those that made them and that trust in them.

(Jasher 11:33)
And when Abram saw all these things his anger was kindled against his father, and he hastened and took a hatchet in his hand, and came to the chamber of the gods, and he broke all his father's gods.

(Jasher 11:34)
And when he had done breaking the images, he placed the hatchet in the hand of the great god which was there before them, and he went out; and Terah his father came home, for he had heard at the door the sound of the striking of the hatchet; so Terah came into the house to know what this was about.

(Jasher 11:35)
And Terah, having heard the noise of the hatchet in the room of images, ran to the room to the images, and he met Abram going out.

(Jasher 11:36)
And Terah entered the room and found all the idols fallen down and broken, and the hatchet in the hand of the largest, which was not broken, and the savory meat which Abram his son had made was still before them.

(Jasher 11:37)
And when Terah saw this his anger was greatly kindled, and he hastened and went from the room to Abram.

(Jasher 11:38)
And he found Abram his son still sitting in the house; and he said to him, What is this work you have done to my gods?

(Jasher 11:39)
And Abram answered Terah his father and he said, Not so my Lord, for I brought savory meat before them, and when I came nigh to them with the meat that they might eat, they all at once stretched forth their hands to eat before the great one had put forth his hand to eat.

(Jasher 11:40)
And the large one saw their works that they did before him, and his anger was violently kindled against them, and he went and took the hatchet that was in the house and came to them and broke them all, and behold the hatchet is yet in his hand as you see.

(Jasher 11:41)
And Terah's anger was kindled against his son Abram, when he spoke this; and Terah said to Abram his son in his anger, What is this tale that you have told? You speak lies to me.

(Jasher 11:42)
Is there in these gods spirit, soul or power to do all you have told me? Are they not wood and stone, and have I not myself made them, and can you speak such lies, saying that the large god that was with them smote them? It is you that placed the hatchet in his hands, and then said he smote them all.

(Jasher 11:43)
And Abram answered his father and said to him, And how can you then serve these idols in whom there is no power to do anything? Can those idols in which you trust deliver you? Can

they hear your prayers when you call upon them? Can they deliver you from the hands of your enemies, or will they fight your battles for you against your enemies, that you should serve wood and stone which can neither speak nor hear?

(Jasher 11:44)
And now surely it is not good for you nor for the sons of men that are connected with you, to do these things; are you so silly, so foolish or so short of understanding that you will serve wood and stone, and do after this manner?

(Jasher 11:45)
And forget the Lord God who made heaven and earth, and Who created you in the earth, and thereby bring a great evil upon your souls in this matter by serving stone and wood?

(Jasher 11:46)
Did not our fathers in days of old sin in this matter, and the Lord God of the universe brought the waters of the flood upon them and destroyed the whole earth?

(Jasher 11:47)
And how can you continue to do this and serve gods of wood and stone, who cannot hear, or speak, or deliver you from oppression, thereby bringing down the anger of the God of the universe upon you?

(Jasher 11:48)
Now therefore my father refrain from this, and bring not evil upon your soul and the souls of your household.

(Jasher 11:49)
And Abram hastened and sprang from before his father, and took the hatchet from his father's largest idol, with which

Abram broke it and ran away.

(Jasher 11:50)
And Terah, seeing all that Abram had done, hastened to go from his house, and he went to the king and he came before Nimrod and stood before him, and he bowed down to the king; and the king said, What do you want?

(Jasher 11:51)
And he said, I beseech you my Lord, to hear me--Now fifty years back a child was born to me, and thus has he done to my gods and thus has he spoken; and now therefore, my Lord and king, send for him that he may come before you, and judge him according to the law, that we may be delivered from his evil.

(Jasher 11:52)
And the king sent three men of his servants, and they went and brought Abram before the king. And Nimrod and all his princes and servants were that day sitting before him, and Terah sat also before them.

(Jasher 11:53)
And the king said to Abram, What is this that you have done to your father and to his gods? And Abram answered the king in the words that he spoke to his father, and he said, The large god that was with them in the house did to them what you have heard.

(Jasher 11:54)
And the king said to Abram, Had they power to speak and eat and do as you have said? And Abram answered the king, saying, And if there be no power in them why do you serve them and cause the sons of men to err through your follies?

(Jasher 11:55)
Do you imagine that they can deliver you or do anything small or great, that you should serve them? And why will you not sense the God of the whole universe, Who created you and in whose power it is to kill and keep alive?

(Jasher 11:56)
O foolish, simple, and ignorant king, woe to you forever.

(Jasher 11:57)
I thought you would teach your servants the upright way, but you have not done this, but have filled the whole earth with your sins and the sins of your people who have followed your ways.

(Jasher 11:58)
Do you not know, or have you not heard, that this evil which you do, our ancestors sinned therein in days of old, and the eternal God brought the waters of the flood upon them and destroyed them all, and also destroyed the whole earth on their account? And will you and your people rise up now and do like to this work, in order to bring down the anger of the Lord God of the universe, and to bring evil upon you and the whole earth?

(Jasher 11:59)
Now therefore put away this evil deed which you do, and serve the God of the universe, as your soul is in His hands, and then it will be well with you.

(Jasher 11:60)
And if your wicked heart will not hearken to my words to cause you to forsake your evil ways, and to serve the eternal God, then will you die in shame in the latter days, you, your people

and all who are connected with you, hearing your words or walking in your evil ways.

(Jasher 11:61)
And when Abram had ceased speaking before the king and princes, Abram lifted up his eyes to the heavens, and he said, The Lord sees all the wicked, and He will judge them.

~ ~ ~

(Jasher 12:1)
And when the king heard the words of Abram he ordered him to be put into prison; and Abram was ten days in prison.

(Jasher 12:2)
And at the end of those days the king ordered that all the kings, princes and governors of different provinces and the sages should come before him, and they sat before him, and Abram was still in the house of confinement.

(Jasher 12:3)
And the king said to the princes and sages, Have you heard what Abram, the son of Terah, has done to his father? Thus has he done to him, and I ordered him to be brought before me, and thus has he spoken; his heart did not misgive him, neither did he stir in my presence, and behold now he is confined in the prison.

(Jasher 12:4)
And therefore, decide what judgment is due to this man who reviled the king; who spoke and did all the things that you heard.

(Jasher 12:5)
And they all answered the king saying, The man who reviles the king should be hanged upon a tree; but having done all the things that he said, and having despised our gods, he must therefore be burned to death, for this is the law in this matter.

(Jasher 12:6)
If it pleases the king to do this, let him order his servants to kindle a fire both night and day in your brick furnace, and then we will cast this man into it. And the king did so, and he commanded his servants that they should prepare a fire for three days and three nights in the king's furnace, that is in Casdim; and the king ordered them to take Abram from prison and bring him out to be burned.

(Jasher 12:7)
And all the king's servants, princes, lords, governors, and judges, and all the inhabitants of the land, about nine hundred thousand men, stood opposite the furnace to see Abram.

(Jasher 12:8)
And all the women and little ones crowded upon the roofs and towers to see what was doing with Abram, and they all stood together at a distance; and there was not a man left that did not come on that day to behold the scene.

(Jasher 12:9)
And when Abram was come, the conjurers of the king and the sages saw Abram, and they cried out to the king, saying, Our sovereign Lord, surely this is the man whom we know to have been the child at whose birth the great star swallowed the four stars, which we declared to the king now fifty years since.

(Jasher 12:10)
And behold now his father has also transgressed your commands, and mocked you by bringing you another child, which you killed.

(Jasher 12:11)
And when the king heard their words, he was exceedingly wroth, and he ordered Terah to be brought before him.

(Jasher 12:12)
And the king said, Have you heard what the conjurers have spoken? Now tell me truly, how you did this; and if you shall speak truth you shall be acquitted.

(Jasher 12:13)
And seeing that the king's anger was so much kindled, Terah said to the king, My Lord and king, you have heard the truth, and what the sages have spoken is right. And the king said, How could you do this thing, to transgress my orders and to give me a child that you did not beget, and to take value for him?

(Jasher 12:14)
And Terah answered the king, Because my tender feelings were excited for my son, at that time, and I took a son of my handmaid, and I brought him to the king.

(Jasher 12:15)
And the king said Who advised you to this? Tell me, do not hide aught from me, and then you shall not die.

(Jasher 12:16)
And Terah was greatly terrified in the king's presence, and he said to the king, It was Haran my eldest son who advised me

to this; and Haran was in those days that Abram was born, two and thirty years old.

(Jasher 12:17)
But Haran did not advise his father to anything, for Terah said this to the king in order to deliver his soul from the king, for he feared greatly; and the king said to Terah, Haran your son who advised you to this shall die through fire with Abram; for the sentence of death is upon him for having rebelled against the king's desire in doing this thing.

(Jasher 12:18)
And Haran at that time felt inclined to follow the ways of Abram, but he kept it within himself.

(Jasher 12:19)
And Haran said in his heart, Behold now the king has seized Abram on account of these things which Abram did, and it shall come to pass, that if Abram prevail over the king I will follow him, but if the king prevail I will go after the king.

(Jasher 12:20)
And when Terah had spoken this to the king concerning Haran his son, the king ordered Haran to be seized with Abram.

(Jasher 12:21)
And they brought them both, Abram and Haran his brother, to cast them into the fire; and all the inhabitants of the land and the king's servants and princes and all the women and little ones were there, standing that day over them.

(Jasher 12:22)
And the king's servants took Abram and his brother, and they stripped them of all their clothes excepting their lower

garments which were upon them.

(Jasher 12:23)
And they bound their hands and feet with linen cords, and the servants of the king lifted them up and cast them both into the furnace.

(Jasher 12:24)
And the Lord loved Abram and he had compassion over him, and the Lord came down and delivered Abram from the fire and he was not burned.

(Jasher 12:25)
But all the cords with which they bound him were burned, while Abram remained and walked about in the fire.

(Jasher 12:26)
And Haran died when they had cast him into the fire, and he was burned to ashes, for his heart was not perfect with the Lord; and those men who cast him into the fire, the flame of the fire spread over them, and they were burned, and twelve men of them died.

(Jasher 12:27)
And Abram walked in the midst of the fire three days and three nights, and all the servants of the king saw him walking in the fire, and they came and told the king, saying, Behold we have seen Abram walking about in the midst of the fire, and even the lower garments which are upon him are not burned, but the cord with which he was bound is burned.

(Jasher 12:28)
And when the king heard their words his heart fainted and he would not believe them; so he sent other faithful princes

to see this matter, and they went and saw it and told it to the king; and the king rose to go and see it, and he saw Abram walking to and fro in the midst of the fire, and he saw Haran's body burned, and the king wondered greatly.

(Jasher 12:29)
And the king ordered Abram to be taken out from the fire; and his servants approached to take him out and they could not, for the fire was round about and the flame ascending toward them from the furnace.

(Jasher 12:30)
And the king's servants fled from it, and the king rebuked them, saying, Make haste and bring Abram out of the fire that you shall not die.

(Jasher 12:31)
And the servants of the king again approached to bring Abram out, and the flames came upon them and burned their faces so that eight of them died.

(Jasher 12:32)
And when the king saw that his servants could not approach the fire lest they should be burned, the king called to Abram, O servant of the God who is in heaven, go forth from amidst the fire and come here before me; and Abram hearkened to the voice of the king, and he went forth from the fire and came and stood before the king.

(Jasher 12:33)
And when Abram came out the king and all his servants saw Abram coming before the king, with his lower garments upon him, for they were not burned, but the cord with which he was bound was burned.

(Jasher 12:34)
And the king said to Abram, How is it that you were not burned in the fire?

(Jasher 12:35)
And Abram said to the king, The God of heaven and earth in Whom I trust and Who has all in His power, He delivered me from the fire into which you cast me.

(Jasher 12:36)
And Haran the brother of Abram was burned to ashes, and they sought for his body, and they found it consumed.

(Genesis 11:28)
And Haran died before his father Terah in the land of his nativity, in Ur of the Chaldees.

(Jasher 12:37)
And Haran was eighty-two years old when he died in the fire of Casdim. And the king, princes, and inhabitants of the land, seeing that Abram was delivered from the fire, they came and bowed down to Abram.

(Jasher 12:38)
And Abram said to them, Do not bow down to me, but bow down to the God of the world Who made you, and serve Him, and go in His ways for it is He who delivered me from out of this fire, and it is He Who created the souls and spirits of all men, and formed man in his mother's womb, and brought him forth into the world, and it is He Who will deliver those who trust in Him from all pain.

(Jasher 12:39)
And this thing seemed very wonderful in the eyes of the king

and princes, that Abram was saved from the fire and that Haran was burned; and the king gave Abram many presents and he gave him his two head servants from the king's house; the name of one was Oni and the name of the other was Eliezer.

(Jasher 12:40)
And all the kings, princes and servants gave Abram many gifts of silver and gold and pearl, and the king and his princes sent him away, and he went in peace.

(Jasher 12:41)
And Abram went forth from the king in peace, and many of the king's servants followed him, and about three hundred men joined him.

(Jasher 12:42)
And Abram returned on that day and went to his father's house, he and the men that followed him, and Abram served the Lord his God all the days of his life, and he walked in his ways and followed his law.

(Jasher 12:43)
And from that day forward Abram inclined the hearts of the sons of men to serve the Lord.

(Jasher 12:45)
And at the expiration of two years from Abram's going out of the fire, that is in the fifty- second year of his life, behold king Nimrod sat in Babel upon the throne, and the king fell asleep and dreamed that he was standing with his troops and hosts in a valley opposite the king's furnace.

(Jasher 12:46)
And he lifted up his eyes and saw a man in the likeness of

Abram coming forth from the furnace, and that he came and stood before the king with his drawn sword, and then sprang to the king with his sword, when the king fled from the man, for he was afraid; and while he was running, the man threw an egg upon the king's head, and the egg became a great river.

(Jasher 12:47)
And the king dreamed that all his troops sank in that river and died, and the king took flight with three men who were before him and he escaped.

(Jasher 12:48)
And the king looked at these men and they were clothed in princely dresses as the garments of kings, and had the appearance and majesty of kings.

(Jasher 12:49)
And while they were running, the river again turned to an egg before the king, and there came forth from the egg a young bird which came before the king, and flew at his head and plucked out the king's eye.

(Jasher 12:50)
And the king was grieved at the sight, and he awoke out of his sleep and his spirit was agitated; and he felt a great terror.

(Jasher 12:51)
And in the morning the king rose from his couch in fear, and he ordered all the wise men and magicians to come before him, when the king related his dream to them.

(Jasher 12:52)
And a wise servant of the king, whose name was Anuki, answered the king, saying, This is nothing else but the evil of

Abram and his seed which will spring up against my Lord and king in the latter days.

(Jasher 12:53)
And behold the day will come when Abram and his seed and the children of his household will war with my king, and they will smite all the king's hosts and his troops.

(Jasher 12:54)
And as to what you have said concerning three men which you saw like to yourself, and which escaped, this means that only you will escape with three kings from the kings of the earth who will be with you in battle.

(Jasher 12:55)
And that which you saw of the river which turned to an egg as at first, and the young bird plucking out your eye, this means nothing else but the seed of Abram which will slay the king in latter days.

(Jasher 12:56)
This is my king's dream, and this is its interpretation, and the dream is true, and the interpretation which your servant has given you is right.

(Jasher 12:57)
Now therefore my king, surely you know that it is now fifty-two years since your sages saw this at the birth of Abram, and if my king will suffer Abram to live in the earth it will be to the injury of my Lord and king, for all the days that Abram lives neither you nor your kingdom will be established, for this was known formerly at his birth; and why will not my king slay him, that his evil may be kept from you in latter days?

(Jasher 12:58)
And Nimrod hearkened to the voice of Anuki, and he sent some of his servants in secret to go and seize Abram, and bring him before the king to suffer death.

(Jasher 12:59)
And Eliezer, Abram's servant whom the king had given him, was at that time in the presence of the king, and he heard what Anuki had advised the king, and what the king had said to cause Abram's death.

(Jasher 12:60)
And Eliezer said to Abram, Hasten, rise up and save your soul, that you may not die through the hands of the king, for thus he saw in a dream concerning you, and thus Anuki interpreted it, and thus also Anuki advised the king concerning you.

(Jasher 12:61)
And Abram hearkened to the voice of Eliezer, and Abram hastened and ran for safety to the house of Noah and his son Shem, and he concealed himself there and found a place of safety; and the king's servants came to Abram's house to seek him, but they could not find him, and they searched throughout the country and he was not to be found, and they went and searched in every direction and he was not to be met with.

(Jasher 12:62)
And when the king's servants could not find Abram they returned to the king, but the king's anger against Abram was stilled, as they did not find him, and the king drove from his mind this matter concerning Abram.

(Jasher 12:63)
And Abram was concealed in Noah's house for one month, until the king had forgotten this matter, but Abram was still afraid of the king; and Terah came to see Abram his son secretly in the house of Noah, and Terah was very great in the eyes of the king.

(Jasher 12:64)
And Abram said to his father, Do you not know that the king thinks to slay me, and to annihilate my name from the earth by the advice of his wicked counselors?

(Jasher 12:65)
Now who do you have here and what do you have in this land? Arise, let us go together to the land of Canaan, that we may be delivered from his hand, lest you perish also through him in the latter days.

(Jasher 12:66)
Do you not know or have you not heard, that it is not through love that Nimrod gives you all this honor, but it is only for his benefit that he bestows all this good upon you?

(Jasher 12:67)
And if he do to you greater good than this, surely these are only vanities of the world, for wealth and riches cannot avail in the day of wrath and anger.

(Jasher 12:68)
Now therefore hearken to my voice, and let us arise and go to the land of Canaan, out of the reach of injury from Nimrod; and serve you the Lord Who created you in the earth and it will be well with you; and cast away all the vain things which you pursue.

(Jasher 12:69)
And Abram ceased to speak, when Noah and his son Shem answered Terah, saying, True is the word which Abram hath said to you.

(Jasher 12:70)
And Terah hearkened to the voice of his son Abram, and Terah did all that Abram said, For this was from the Lord, that the king should not cause Abram's death.

(Genesis 11:31) (Jasher 13:1) (Jubilees 12:15)
And Terah took Abram his son, and Lot the son of Haran his son's son, and Sarai his daughter in law, his son Abram's wife; and all the souls of his household and they went forth with them from Ur of the Chaldees, to go into the land of Lebanon and into the land of Canaan; and they came to Haran, and dwelt there for it was exceedingly good land for pasture, and of sufficient extent for those who accompanied them. And Abram dwelt with Terah his father in Haran two weeks of years.

(Jubilees 12:16)
And in the sixth week, in the fifth year thereof, Abram sat up throughout the night on the new moon of the seventh month to observe the stars from the evening to the morning, in order to see what would be the character of the year with regard to the rains, and he was alone as he sat and observed.

(Jubilees 12:17)
And a word came into his heart and he said: All the signs of the stars, and the signs of the moon and of the sun are all in the hand of the Lord. Why do I search them out?

(Jubilees 12:18)
If He desires, He causes it to rain, morning and evening; And if He desires, He withholds it, And all things are in his hand.

(Jubilees 12:19)
And he prayed that night and said, My God, God Most High, You alone are my God, And You and Your dominion have I chosen. And You have created all things, And all things that are the work of your hands.

(Jubilees 12:20)
Deliver me from the hands of evil spirits who have dominion over the thoughts of men's hearts, And let them not lead me astray from You, my God. And establish me and my seed forever that we go not astray from here after, and forevermore.

(Jubilees 12:21)
And he said, Shall I return to Ur of the Chaldees who seek my face that I may return to them, am I to remain here in this place? The right path before You prosper it in the hands of Your servant that he may fulfill it and that I may not walk in the deceitfulness of my heart, O my God.

(Jubilees 12:22)
And he made an end of speaking and praying, and behold the word of the Lord was sent to him through me, saying: Get you up from your country, and from your kindred and from the house of your father to a land which I will show you, and I shall make you a great and numerous nation.

(Jubilees 12:23)
And I will bless you And I will make your name great, And you shall be blessed in the earth, And in You shall all families of the earth be blessed, And I will bless them that bless you, And

curse them that curse you.

(Jubilees 12:24)
And I will be a God to you and your son, and to your son's son, and to all your seed: fear not, from here after, and to all generations of the earth I am your God.

(Jubilees 12:25)
And the Lord God said: Open his mouth and his ears, that he may hear and speak with his mouth, with the language which has been revealed; for it had ceased from the mouths of all the children of men from the day of the overthrow of Babel.

(Jubilees 12:26)
And I opened his mouth, and his ears and his lips, and I began to speak with him in Hebrew in the tongue of the creation.

(Jubilees 12:27)
And he took the books of his fathers, and these were written in Hebrew, and he transcribed them, and he began from here after, to study them, and I made known to him that which he could not (understand), and he studied them during the six rainy months.

~ ~ ~

(Jasher 13:2)
And the people of the land of Haran saw that Abram was good and upright with God and men, and that the Lord his God was with him, and some of the people of the land of Haran came and joined Abram, and he taught them the instruction of the Lord and his ways; and these men remained with Abram in

his house and they adhered to him.

(Jasher 13:3)
And Abram remained in the land three years, and at the expiration of three years the Lord appeared to Abram and said to him; I am the Lord who brought you forth from Ur Casdim, and delivered you from the hands of all your enemies.

(Jasher 13:4)
And now therefore if you will hearken to my voice and keep my commandments, my statutes and my laws, then will I cause your enemies to fall before you, and I will multiply your seed like the stars of heaven, and I will send my blessing upon all the works of your hands, and you shall lack nothing.

(Jasher 13:5...)
Arise now, take your wife and all belonging to you and go to the land of Canaan and remain there, and I will there be to you for a God, and I will bless you.

~ ~ ~

(Jubilees 12:28)
And it came to pass in the seventh year of the sixth week that he spoke to his father and informed him, that he would leave Haran to go into the land of Canaan to see it and return to him.

(Jubilees 12:29)
And Terah his father said to him; Go in peace: May the eternal God make your path straight. And the Lord be with you, and protect you from all evil, And grant to you grace, mercy and

favor before those who see you, And may none of the children of men have power over you to harm you; Go in peace.

(Jubilees 12:30)
And if you see a land pleasant to your eyes to dwell in, then arise and take me to you and take Lot with you, the son of Haran your brother as your own son: the Lord be with you.

(Jubilees 12:31)
And Nahor your brother leave with me till you return in peace, and we go with you all together.

~ ~ ~

(...Jasher 13:5)
And Abram rose and took his wife and all belonging to him, and he went to the land of Canaan as the Lord had told him; and Abram was fifty years old when he went from Haran.

(Jasher 13:6)
And Abram came to the land of Canaan and dwelt in the midst of the city, and he there pitched his tent among the children of Canaan, inhabitants of the land.

(Jasher 13:7)
And the Lord appeared to Abram when he came to the land of Canaan, and said to him, This is the land which I gave to you and to your seed after you forever, and I will make your seed like the stars of heaven, and I will give to your seed for an inheritance all the lands which you see.

(Jasher 13:8)
And Abram built an altar in the place where God had spoken to him, and Abram there called upon the name of the Lord.

(Jasher 13:9)
At that time, at the end of three years of Abram's dwelling in the land of Canaan, in that year Noah died, which was the fifty-eighth year of the life of Abram; and all the days that Noah lived were nine hundred and fifty years and he died.

(Jasher 13:10)
And Abram dwelt in the land of Canaan, he, his wife, and all belonging to him, and all those that accompanied him, together with those that joined him from the people of the land; but Nahor, Abram's brother, and Terah his father, and Lot the son of Haran and all belonging to them dwelt in Haran.

(Jasher 13:11)
In the fifth year of Abram's dwelling in the land of Canaan the people of Sodom and Gomorrah and all the cities of the plain revolted from the power of Chedorlaomer, king of Elam; for all the kings of the cities of the plain had served Chedorlaomer for twelve years, and given him a yearly tax, but in those days in the thirteenth year, they rebelled against him.

(Jasher 13:12)
And in the tenth year of Abram's dwelling in the land of Canaan there was war between Nimrod king of Shinar and Chedorlaomer king of Elam, and Nimrod came to fight with Chedorlaomer and to subdue him.

(Jasher 13:13)
For Chedorlaomer was at that time one of the princes of the hosts of Nimrod, and when all the people at the tower were

dispersed and those that remained were also scattered upon the face of the earth, Chedorlaomer went to the land of Elam and reigned over it and rebelled against his Lord.

(Jasher 13:14)
And in those days when Nimrod saw that the cities of the plain had rebelled, he came with pride and anger to war with Chedorlaomer, and Nimrod assembled all his princes and subjects, about seven hundred thousand men, and went against Chedorlaomer, and Chedorlaomer went out to meet him with five thousand men, and they prepared for battle in the valley of Babel which is between Elam and Shinar.

(Jasher 13:15)
And all those kings fought there, and Nimrod and his people were smitten before the people of Chedorlaomer, and there fell from Nimrod's men about six hundred thousand, and Mardon the king's son fell among them.

(Jasher 13:16)
And Nimrod fled and returned in shame and disgrace to his land, and he was under subjection to Chedorlaomer for a long time, and Chedorlaomer returned to his land and sent princes of his host to the kings that dwelt around him, to Arioch king of Elasar, and to Tidal king of Goyim, and made a covenant with them, and they were all obedient to his commands.

(Jasher 13:17)
And it was in the fifteenth year of Abram's dwelling in the land of Canaan, which is the seventieth year of the life of Abram, and the Lord appeared to Abram in that year and he said to him, I am the Lord who brought you out from Ur Casdim to give you this land for an inheritance.

(Jasher 13:18)
Now therefore walk before me and be perfect and keep my commands, for to you and to your seed I will give this land for an inheritance, from the river Mitzraim to the great river Euphrates.

(Jasher 13:19)
And you shall come to your fathers in peace and in good age, and the fourth generation shall return here in this land and shall inherit it forever; and Abram built an altar, and he called upon the name of the Lord who appeared to him, and he brought up sacrifices upon the altar to the Lord.

(Jasher 13:20)
At that time Abram returned and went to Haran to see his father and mother, and his father's household, and Abram and his wife and all belonging to him returned to Haran, and Abram dwelt in Haran five years.

(Jasher 13:21)
And many of the people of Haran, about seventy-two men, followed Abram and Abram taught them the instruction of the Lord and his ways, and he taught them to know the Lord.

(Genesis 11:32)

And the days of Terah were two hundred and five years: and Terah died in Haran.

Genesis: Chapter Twelve

(Genesis 12:1) (Jasher 13:22, 23...)

In those days, the Lord appeared to Abram in Haran, and the Lord had said to him, Behold, I spoke to you these twenty years back, Get out of your country, from your birth-place and from your kindred, and from your father's house, to a land that I will show you: to give it to you and to your children.

(Genesis 12:2) (...Jasher 13:23)

For there in that land, I will make of you a great nation, and I will bless you, and make your name great; and you shall be a blessing to the families of the earth:

(Genesis 12:3)

And I will bless them that bless you, and curse him that curses you: and in you shall all families of the earth be blessed.

(Jasher 13:24)

Now therefore arise, go forth from this place, you, your wife, and all belonging to you, also everyone born in your house and all the souls you have made in Haran, and bring them out with you from here, and rise to return to the land of Canaan.

(Genesis 12:4) (...Jasher 13:26)

So Abram departed, as the Lord had spoken to him; and Lot went with him: and Abram was seventy five years old when he departed out of Haran to return to the land of Canaan.

(Genesis 12:5) (Jasher 13:25, 26...) (Jubilees 13:1...)

And Abram arose and journeyed from Haran, and Abram

took Sarai his wife, and Lot his brother's son, and all their substance that they had gathered, and all that were born to him in his house and the souls that they had gotten in Haran; and they went forth to go to the land of Canaan according to the word of the Lord; and into the land of Canaan they came.

(Genesis 12:6) (Jasher 13:27) (...Jubilees 13:1)
And he came to the land of Canaan according to the word of the Lord to Abram. And Abram passed through the land and he came into Asshur, and proceeded to the place of Sichem, to the plain of Moreh and he pitched his tent and dwelt near a lofty oak, and with him was Lot his brother's son, and all belonging to him. And the Canaanite was then in the land.

(Jubilees 13:2)
And he saw, and, behold, the land was very pleasant from the entering of Hamath to the lofty oak.

(Genesis 12:7) (Jasher 13:28) (Jubilees 13:3, 4)
And the Lord appeared to Abram again, and said, To you and to your seed I will give this land: and he built an altar there and he offered thereon a burnt sacrifice to the Lord, who appeared to him which is still to this day in the plains of Mamre.

(Genesis 12:8...) (Jubilees 13:5)
And he removed from there to a mountain on the east of Bethel, and pitched his tent, having Bethel on the west, and Hai on the east:

(Jubilees 13:6)
And he saw and behold, the land was very wide and good, and everything grew thereon - vines and figs and pomegranates, oaks and ilexes, and terebinths and oil trees, and cedars and cypresses and date trees, and all trees of the field, and there

was water on the mountains.

(Jubilees 13:7)
And he blessed the Lord who had led him out of Ur of the Chaldees, and had brought him to this land.

(...Genesis 12:8) (Jubilees 13:8)
And it came to pass in the first year, in the seventh week, on the new moon of the first month, that there he built an altar to the Lord on this mountain, and called on the name of the Lord: You, the eternal God, are my God.

(Jubilees 13:9)
And he offered on the altar a burnt sacrifice to the Lord that He should be with him and not forsake him all the days of his life.

(Genesis 12:9) (Jubilees 13:10,11...)
And he removed from there and Abram journeyed, going on still toward the south. And he came to Hebron and Hebron was built at that time, and he dwelt there two years, and he went into the land of the south, to Bealoth.

(Jasher 14:1)
In those days, there was in the land of Shinar a wise man who had understanding in all wisdom, and of a beautiful appearance, but he was poor and indigent; his name was Rikayon and he was hard set to support himself.

(Jasher 14:2)
And he resolved to go to Egypt, to Oswiris the son of Anom king of Egypt, to show the king his wisdom; for perhaps he might find grace in his sight, to raise him up and give him maintenance; and Rikayon did so.

(Jasher 14:3)
And when Rikayon came to Egypt he asked the inhabitants of Egypt concerning the king, and the inhabitants of Egypt told him the custom of the king of Egypt, for it was then the custom of the king of Egypt that he went from his royal palace and was seen abroad only one day in the year, and after that the king would return to his palace to remain there.

(Jasher 14:4)
And on the day when the king went forth he passed judgment in the land, and everyone having a suit came before the king that day to obtain his request.

(Jasher 14:5)
And when Rikayon heard of the custom in Egypt and that he could not come into the presence of the king, he grieved greatly and was very sorrowful.

(Jasher 14:6)
And in the evening Rikayon went out and found a house in ruins, formerly a bake house in Egypt, and he abode there all night in bitterness of soul and pinched with hunger, and sleep was removed from his eyes.

(Jasher 14:7)
And Rikayon considered within himself what he should do in the town until the king made his appearance, and how he might maintain himself there.

(Jasher 14:8)
And he rose in the morning and walked about, and met in his way those who sold vegetables and various sorts of seed with which they supplied the inhabitants.

(Jasher 14:9)
And Rikayon wished to do the same in order to get a maintenance in the city, but he was unacquainted with the custom of the people, and he was like a blind man among them.

(Jasher 14:10)
And he went and obtained vegetables to sell them for his support, and the rabble assembled about him and ridiculed him, and took his vegetables from him and left him nothing.

(Jasher 14:11)
And he rose up from there in bitterness of soul, and went sighing to the bake house in which he had remained all the night before, and he slept there the second night.

(Jasher 14:12)
And on that night again he reasoned within himself how he could save himself from starvation, and he devised a scheme how to act.

(Jasher 14:13)
And he rose up in the morning and acted ingeniously, and went and hired thirty strong men of the rabble, carrying their war instruments in their hands, and he led them to the top of the Egyptian sepulcher, and he placed them there.

(Jasher 14:14)
And he commanded them, saying, Thus says the king, Strengthen yourselves and be valiant men, and let no man be buried here until two hundred pieces of silver be given, and then he may be buried; and those men did according to the order of Rikayon to the people of Egypt the whole of that year.

(Jasher 14:15)
And in eight months time Rikayon and his men gathered great riches of silver and gold, and Rikayon took a great quantity of horses and other animals, and he hired more men, and he gave them horses and they remained with him.

(Jasher 14:16)
And when the year came around, at the time the king went forth into the town, all the inhabitants of Egypt assembled together to speak to him concerning the work of Rikayon and his men.

(Jasher 14:17)
And the king went forth on the appointed day, and all the Egyptians came before him and cried to him, saying,

(Jasher 14:18)
May the king live forever. What is this thing you do in the town to your servants, not to suffer a dead body to be buried until so much silver and gold be given? Was there ever the like to this done in the whole earth, from the days of former kings yea even from the days of Adam, to this day, that the dead should not be buried only for a set price?

(Jasher 14:19)
We know it to be the custom of kings to take a yearly tax from the living, but you do not only do this, but from the dead also you exact a tax day by day.

(Jasher 14:20)
Now, O king, we can no more bear this, for the whole city is ruined on this account, and do you not know it?

(Jasher 14:21)
And when the king heard all that they had spoken he was very wroth, and his anger burned within him at this affair, for he had known nothing of it.

(Jasher 14:22)
And the king said, Who and where is he that dares to do this wicked thing in my land without my command? Surely you will tell me.

(Jasher 14:23)
And they told him all the works of Rikayon and his men, and the king's anger was aroused, and he ordered Rikayon and his men to be brought before him.

(Jasher 14:24)
And Rikayon took about a thousand children, sons and daughters, and clothed them in silk and embroidery, and he set them upon horses and sent them to the king by means of his men, and he also took a great quantity of silver and gold and precious stones, and a strong and beautiful horse, as a present for the king, with which he came before the king and bowed down to the earth before him; and the king, his servants and all the inhabitants of Egypt wondered at the work of Rikayon, and they saw his riches and the present that he had brought to the king.

(Jasher 14:25)
And it greatly pleased the king and he wondered at it; and when Rikayon sat before him the king asked him concerning all his works, and Rikayon spoke all his words wisely before the king, his servants and all the inhabitants of Egypt.

(Jasher 14:26)
And when the king heard the words of Rikayon and his wisdom, Rikayon found grace in his sight, and he met with grace and kindness from all the servants of the king and from all the inhabitants of Egypt, on account of his wisdom and excellent speeches, and from that time they loved him exceedingly.

(Jasher 14:27)
And the king answered and said to Rikayon, Your name shall no more be called Rikayon but Pharaoh shall be your name, since you exacted a tax from the dead; and he called his name Pharaoh.

(Jasher 14:28)
And the king and his subjects loved Rikayon for his wisdom, and they consulted with all the inhabitants of Egypt to make him prefect under the king.

(Jasher 14:29)
And all the inhabitants of Egypt and its wise men did so, and it was made a law in Egypt.

(Jasher 14:30)
And they made Rikayon Pharaoh prefect under Oswiris king of Egypt, and Rikayon Pharaoh governed over Egypt, daily administering justice to the whole city, but Oswiris the king would judge the people of the land one day in the year, when he went out to make his appearance.

(Jasher 14:31)
And Rikayon Pharaoh cunningly usurped the government of Egypt, and he exacted a tax from all the inhabitants of Egypt.

(Jasher 14:32)
And all the inhabitants of Egypt greatly loved Rikayon Pharaoh, and they made a decree to call every king that should reign over them and their seed in Egypt, Pharaoh.

(Jasher 14:33)
Therefore, all the kings that reigned in Egypt from that time forward were called Pharaoh to this day.

(Genesis 12:10) (Jasher 15:1, 2) (...Jubilees 13:11...)
And in that year, there was a heavy famine in the land of Canaan: and the inhabitants of the land could not remain on account of the famine for it was very grievous. And Abram and all belonging to him rose and went down into Egypt, in the third year of the week, to sojourn there; for the famine was grievous in the land. And when they were at the brook Mitzraim they remained there some time to rest from the fatigue of the road.

(...Jubilees 13:11)
And he dwelt in Egypt five years before his wife was torn away from him.

(Jubilees 13:12)
Now Tanais in Egypt was at that time built - seven years after Hebron.

(Jasher 15:3)
And Abram and Sarai were walking at the border of the brook Mitzraim, and Abram beheld his wife Sarai that she was very beautiful.

(Genesis 12:11) (Jasher 15:4...)
And it came to pass, when he was come near to enter into

Egypt, that he said to Sarai his wife, Behold now, I know that you are a fair woman to look on since God has created you with such a beautiful countenance.

(Genesis 12:12) (...Jasher 15:4)

Therefore, it shall come to pass, when the Egyptians shall see you, that they shall say, This is his wife: and I am afraid of the Egyptians lest they will kill me, but they will save you alive and take you away, for the fear of God is not in these places.

(Genesis 12:13) (Jasher 15:5)

Surely then you shall do this, Say, I pray, you are my sister to all that may ask you: that it may be well with me for your sake; and my soul shall live because of you and not be put to death.

(Jasher 15:6)

And Abram commanded the same to all those that came with him to Egypt on account of the famine; also his nephew Lot he commanded, saying, If the Egyptians ask you concerning Sarai say she is the sister of Abram.

(Jasher 15:7)

And yet with all these orders Abram did not put confidence in them, but he took Sarai and placed her in a chest and concealed it among their vessels, for Abram was greatly concerned about Sarai on account of the wickedness of the Egyptians.

(Jasher 15:8)

And Abram and all belonging to him rose up from the brook Mitzraim and came to Egypt; and they had scarcely entered the gates of the city when the guards stood up to them saying, Give tithe to the king from what you have, and then you may come into the town; and Abram and those that were with him did so.

(Jasher 15:9)
And Abram with the people that were with him came to Egypt, and when they came they brought the chest in which Sarai was concealed and the Egyptians saw the chest.

(Jasher 15:10)
And the king's servants approached Abram, saying, What do you have here in this chest which we have not seen? Now open you the chest and give tithe to the king of all that it contains.

(Jasher 15:11)
And Abram said, This chest I will not open, but all you demand upon it I will give. And Pharaoh's officers answered Abram, saying, It is a chest of precious stones, give us the tenth thereof.

(Jasher 15:12)
Abram said, All that you desire I will give, but you must not open the chest.

(Genesis 12:14) (Jasher 15:13)
And it came to pass, that, when Abram was come into Egypt, the king's officers pressed Abram, and they reached the chest and opened it with force, and the Egyptians beheld the beautiful woman in the chest that she was very fair.

(Genesis 12:15...) (Jasher 15:14)
And the when princes also of Pharaoh saw Sarai, they were struck with admiration at her beauty, and all the princes and servants of Pharaoh assembled to see Sarai, for she was very beautiful. And the king's officers ran and told Pharaoh all that they had seen and commended her before Pharaoh: and Pharaoh ordered her to be brought, and the woman came before the king.

(Jasher 15:15)
And Pharaoh beheld Sarai and she pleased him exceedingly, and he was struck with her beauty, and the king rejoiced greatly on her account, and made presents to those who brought him the tidings concerning her.

(...Genesis 12:15) (Jasher 15:16)
And the woman was then taken into Pharaoh's house. And Abram grieved on account of his wife, and he prayed to the Lord to deliver her from the hands of Pharaoh.

(Jasher 15:17)
And Sarai also prayed at that time and said, O Lord God, You told my Lord Abram to go from his land and from his father's house to the land of Canaan, and You promised to do well with him if he would perform Your commands; now behold we have done that which You commanded us, and we left our land and our families, and we went to a strange land and to a people whom we have not known before.

(Jasher 15:18)
And we came to this land to avoid the famine, and this evil accident has befallen me; now therefore, O Lord God, deliver us and save us from the hand of this oppressor, and do well with me for the sake of your mercy.

(Jasher 15:19)
And the Lord hearkened to the voice of Sarai, and the Lord sent an angel to deliver Sarai from the power of Pharaoh.

(Jasher 15:20)
And the king came and sat before Sarai and behold an angel of the Lord was standing over them, and he appeared to Sarai and said to her, Do not fear, for the Lord has heard your prayer.

(Jasher 15:21)
And the king approached Sarai and said to her, What is that man to you who brought you here? And she said, He is my brother.

(Jasher 15:22...)
And the king said, It is incumbent upon us to make him great, to elevate him and to do to him all the good which you shall command us;

(Genesis 12:16) (...Jasher 15:22)
And at that time, the king entreated Abram well for her sake and he sent to Abram silver and gold and precious stones in abundance: and he had sheep, and oxen, and he donkeys, and men servants, and maidservants, and she donkeys, and camels. And the king ordered Abram to be brought, and he sat in the court of the king's house, and the king greatly exalted Abram on that night.

(Genesis 12:17) (Jubilees 13:13)
And it came to pass when Pharaoh seized Sarai, the wife of Abram that the Lord plagued Pharaoh and his house with great plagues because of Sarai Abram's wife.

(Jasher 15:23)
And the king approached to speak to Sarai, and he reached out his hand to touch her, when the angel smote him heavily, and he was terrified and he refrained from reaching to her.

(Jasher 15:24)
And when the king came near to Sarai, the angel smote him to the ground, and acted thus to him the whole night, and the king was terrified.

(Jasher 15:25)
And the angel on that night smote heavily all the servants of the king, and his whole household, on account of Sarai, and there was a great lamentation that night among the people of Pharaoh's house.

(Jasher 15:26)
And Pharaoh, seeing the evil that befell him, said, Surely, on account of this woman has this thing happened to me, and he removed himself at some distance from her and spoke pleasing words to her.

(Jasher 15:27)
And the king said to Sarai, Tell me I pray you concerning the man whom you came here with; and Sarai said, This man is my husband, and I said to you that he was my brother for I was afraid, lest you should put him to death through wickedness.

(Jasher 15:28)
And the king kept away from Sarai, and the plagues of the angel of the Lord ceased from him and his household; and Pharaoh knew that he was smitten on account of Sarai, and the king was greatly astonished at this.

(Genesis 12:18) (Jasher 15:29...)
And in the morning Pharaoh called Abram, and said to him, What is this that you have done to me? Why did you not tell me that she was your wife?

(Genesis 12:19) (...Jasher 15:29, 30...)
Why did you say, She is my sister? So I might have taken her to me to wife: and this heavy plague has therefore come upon me and my household. Now therefore behold your wife,

take her, and go your way from our land lest we all die on her account.

(...Jasher 15:30) (Jubilees 13:15...)
And Pharaoh took more cattle, men servants and maid servants, and silver and gold, to give to Abram. And Pharaoh gave back Sarai, the wife of Abram.

(Jasher 15:31)
And the king took a maiden whom he begot by his concubines, and he gave her to Sarai for a handmaid.

(Jasher 15:32)
And the king said to his daughter, It is better for you my daughter to be a handmaid in this man's house than to be mistress in my house, after we have beheld the evil that befell us on account of this woman.

(...Jubilees 13:15)
And the king sent Abram out of the land of Egypt.

(Genesis 12:20) (Jasher 15:33)
And Abram arose, and he and all belonging to him went away from Egypt; And Pharaoh commanded some of his men concerning him to accompany him and all that went with him: and they sent him away, and his wife, and all that he had.

Genesis: Chapter Thirteen

(Genesis 13:1) (Jasher 15:34)

And Abram went up out of Egypt, and returned to the land of Canaan, to the place where he had made the altar, where he at first had pitched his tent. He, and his wife, and all that he had, and Lot with him, into the south.

(Genesis 13:2) (Jubilees 13:14...)

And Abram was very rich in sheep, in cattle, in donkeys, and horses, and camels, and menservants, and maidservants, and in silver, and in gold exceedingly.

(Genesis 13:3) (Jubilees 13:15...)

And Abram went on his journeys from the south even to Bethel, to the place where his tent had been at the beginning, between Bethel and Hai;

(Genesis 13:4) (...Jubilees 13:15)

To the place of the altar, which he had made there at the first with Ai on the east, and Bethel on the west: and there Abram called on the name of the Lord and he blessed the Lord his God who had brought him back in peace.

(Jubilees 13:16)

And it came to pass in the forty-first jubilee in the third year of the first week, that he returned to this place and offered thereon a burnt sacrifice, and called on the name of the Lord, and said: You, the Most High God, are my God forever and ever.

(Genesis 13:5) (Jasher 15:35) (...Jubilees 13:14)
And Lot also, the son of Haran, Abram's brother, which went with Abram, was wealthy; he had a heavy stock of cattle, flocks, and herds, and tents, for the Lord was bountiful to them on account of Abram.

(Genesis 13:6) (Jasher 15:36...)
And when Abram was dwelling in the land, the land was not able to bear them on account of their cattle, that they might dwell together: for their substance was great, so that they could not dwell together.

(Genesis 13:7) (...Jasher 15:36)
And there was a strife between the herdsmen of Abram's cattle and the herdsmen of Lot's cattle: and the Canaanite and the Perizzite dwelt then in the land.

(Jasher 15:37)
And when Abram's herdsmen went to feed their flock they would not go into the fields of the people of the land, but the cattle of Lot's herdsmen did otherwise, for they were suffered to feed in the fields of the people of the land.

(Jasher 15:38)
And the people of the land saw this occurrence daily, and they came to Abram and quarreled with him on account of Lot's herdsmen.

(Jasher 15:39)
And Abram said to Lot, What is this you are doing to me, to make me despicable to the inhabitants of the land, that you order your herdsman to feed your cattle in the fields of other people? Do you not know that I am a stranger in this land among the children of Canaan, and why will you do this to me?

(Jasher 15:40)
And Abram quarreled daily with Lot on account of this, but Lot would not listen to Abram, and he continued to do the same and the inhabitants of the land came and told Abram.

(Genesis 13:8) (Jasher 15:41)
And Abram said to Lot, How long will you be to me for a stumbling block with the inhabitants of the land? Now Let there be no strife, I pray, between me and you, and between my herdsmen and your herdsmen; for we be brethren.

(Genesis 13:9) (Jasher 15:42)
Is not the whole land before you? Separate yourself, I pray, from me: go and choose a place where you may dwell with your cattle and all belonging to you, but Keep yourself at a distance from me, you and your household. If you will take the left hand, then I will go to the right; or if you depart to the right hand, then I will go to the left.

(Jasher 15:43)
And be not afraid in going from me, for if any one do an injury to you, let me know and I will avenge your cause from him, only remove from me.

(Genesis 13:10) (Jasher 15:44, 45)
And when Abram had spoken all these words to Lot, then Lot arose and lifted up his eyes, and beheld all the plain of Jordan. And he saw that it was well watered everywhere, and good for man as well as affording pasture for the cattle - before the Lord destroyed Sodom and Gomorrah, even as the garden of the Lord, like the land of Egypt, as you come to Zoar.

(Genesis 13:11) (Jasher 15:46...) (Jubilees 13:17...)
And in the fourth year of this week, then Lot chose him all the

plain of Jordan; and Lot went from Abram, and he journeyed east to that place: and they separated themselves the one from the other.

(Genesis 13:12) (...Jasher 15:46) (...Jubilees 13:17...)
Abram dwelt in the land of Canaan, and Lot dwelt in the cities of the plain, and pitched his tent toward Sodom. And Lot dwelt in Sodom.

(Genesis 13:13) (...Jubilees 13:17)
But the men of Sodom were wicked and sinners before the Lord exceedingly.

(Jubilees 13:18)
And it grieved him in his heart that his brother's son had parted from him; for he had no children.

(Genesis 13:14) (Jubilees 13:19)
And in that year when Lot was taken captive, the Lord said to Abram, after that Lot was separated from him, in the fourth year of this week: Lift up now your eyes, and look from the place where you are dwelling northward, and southward, and eastward, and westward:

(Genesis 13:15) (Jubilees 13:20...)
For all the land which you see, will I give it to you, and to your seed forever.

(Genesis 13:16) (...Jubilees 13:20)
And I will make your seed as the dust of the earth, as the sand of the sea so that if a man can number the dust of the earth, then your seed shall also not be numbered.

(Genesis 13:17) (Jubilees 13:21...)

Arise, walk through the land in the length of it and in the width of it, and see it all; for I will give it to you, and to your seed.

(Genesis 13:18) (Jasher 15:47) (...Jubilees 13:21)

Then Abram removed his tent, and came and dwelt in the plain of Mamre, which is in Hebron, and he pitched his tent there, and Abram remained in that place many years, and built an altar to the Lord there.

Genesis: Chapter Fourteen

(Genesis 14:1)
And it came to pass in the days of Amraphel king of Shinar, Arioch king of Ellasar, Chedorlaomer king of Elam, and Tidal king of nations;

(Genesis 14:2)
That these made war with Bera king of Sodom, and with Birsha king of Gomorrah, Shinab king of Admah, and Shemeber king of Zeboiim, and the king of Bela, which is Zoar.

(Jasher 16:1)
At that time Chedorlaomer king of Elam sent to all the neighboring kings, to Nimrod, king of Shinar who was then under his power, and to Tidal, king of Goyim, and to Arioch, king of Elasar, with whom he made a covenant, saying, Come up to me and assist me, that we may smite all the towns of Sodom and its inhabitants, for they have rebelled against me these thirteen years.

(Jasher 16:2)
And these four kings went up with all their camps, about eight hundred thousand men, and they went as they were, and smote every man they found in their road.

(Genesis 14:3) (Jasher 16:3)
And the five kings of Sodom and Gomorrah, Shinab king of Admah, Shemeber king of Zeboyim, Bera king of Sodom, Bersha king of Gomorrah, and Bela king of Zoar, went out to meet them, and all these were joined together in the vale of Siddim, which is the salt sea.

(Genesis 14:4)
Twelve years they served Chedorlaomer, and in the thirteenth year they rebelled.

(Genesis 14:5)
And in the fourteenth year Chedorlaomer came, and the kings that were with him, and smote the Rephaims in Ashteroth Karnaim, and the Zuzims in Ham, and the Emims in Shaveh Kiriathaim,

(Genesis 14:6)
And the Horites in their Mount Seir, to Elparan, which is by the wilderness.

(Genesis 14:7)
And they returned, and came to Enmishpat, which is Kadesh, and smote all the country of the Amalekites, and also the Amorites, that dwelt in Hazezontamar.

(Genesis 14:8)
And there went out the king of Sodom, and the king of Gomorrah, and the king of Admah, and the king of Zeboiim, and the king of Bela (the same is Zoar;) and they joined battle with them in the vale of Siddim;

(Genesis 14:9)
With Chedorlaomer the king of Elam, and with Tidal king of nations, and Amraphel king of Shinar, and Arioch king of Ellasar; four kings with five.

(Jasher 16:4)
And these nine kings made war in the valley of Siddim; and the kings of Sodom and Gomorrah were smitten before the kings of Elam.

(Jubilees 13:22)
And in this year, Chedorlaomer, king of Elam, and Amraphel, king of Shinar, and Arioch king of Sellasar, and Tergal, king of nations, came and slew the king of Gomorrah, and the king of Sodom fled, and many fell through wounds in the vale of Siddim, by the Salt Sea.

(Genesis 14:10) (Jasher 16:5...)
And the vale of Siddim was full of slime pits; and the kings of Elam pursued the kings of Sodom, and the kings of Sodom and Gomorrah with their camps fled, and fell there; and they that remained fled to the mountain for safety.

(Genesis 14:11) (...Jasher 16:5)
And the five kings of Elam came after them and pursued them to the gates of Sodom, and they took all the goods of Sodom and Gomorrah, and all their victuals, and went their way.

(Genesis 14:12) (Jasher 16:6...) (Jubilees 13:23)
And they plundered all the cities of Sodom and Gomorrah. And they took captive Sodom and Adam and Zeboim, and they also took captive Lot, Abram's brother's son, who dwelt in Sodom, and his goods, and they seized all the goods of the cities of Sodom, and they departed to Dan.

(Genesis 14:13) (...Jasher 16:6) (Jubilees 13:24...)
And there came one that had escaped, Unic, Abram's servant, who was in the battle, saw this, and told Abram the Hebrew all that the kings had done to the cities of Sodom, and that Lot his brother's son was taken captive by them; for he dwelt in the plain of Mamre the Amorite, brother of Eshcol, and brother of Aner: and these were confederate with Abram.

(Genesis 14:14) (Jasher 16:7...) (...Jubilees 13:24)

And when Abram heard that his brother was taken captive, he rose up with about three hundred and eighteen men that were with him, and he armed his trained, household servants, born in his own house, and he pursued these kings to Dan.

(Genesis 14:15) (...Jasher 16:7)

And he divided himself against them, he and his servants, by night, and smote them, and pursued them to Hobah, which is on the left hand of Damascus. And they all fell before Abram and his men, and there was none remaining but the four kings who fled, and they went each his own road.

(Genesis 14:16) (Jasher 16:8)

And Abram recovered and he brought back all the goods of Sodom, and also brought again his brother Lot, and his goods, and the women also, and little ones and all belonging to him and the people, so that Lot lacked nothing.

(Jasher 16:9)

And when he returned from smiting these kings, he and his men passed the valley of Siddim where the kings had made war together.

(Genesis 14:17) (Jasher 16:10)

And Bera the king of Sodom, and the rest of his men that were with him, went out from the lime pits into which they had fallen, to meet Abram and his men after his return from the slaughter of Chedorlaomer, and of the kings that were with him, at the valley of Shaveh, which is the king's dale.

(Genesis 14:18) (Jasher 16:11)

And Melchizedek, king of Salem, the same was Shem, went out with his men to meet Abram and his people, brought forth bread and wine, and they remained together in the valley of Melech: and he was the priest of the Most High God.

(Genesis 14:19) (Jasher 16:12...)
And he blessed Abram, and said, Blessed be Abram of the Most High God, Possessor of heaven and earth:

(Genesis 14:20) (...Jasher 16:12)
And blessed be the Most High God, which has delivered your enemies into your hand. And Abram gave him a tenth from all that he had brought from the spoil of his enemies, for Adonizedek was a priest before God.

(Jubilees 13:25)
For Abram, and for his seed, a tenth of the first fruits to the Lord, and the Lord ordained it as an ordinance forever that they should give it to the priests who served before Him, that they should possess it forever.

(Jubilees 13:26)
And to this law there is no limit of days; for He has ordained it for the generations forever that they should give to the Lord the tenth of everything, of the seed and of the wine and of the oil and of the cattle and of the sheep.

(Jubilees 13:27)
And He gave it to His priests to eat and to drink with joy before Him.

(Genesis 14:21) (Jasher 16:13) (Jubilees 13:28)
And all the kings of Sodom and Gomorrah who were there, with their servants, approached Abram and bowed himself before him and begged of him to return them their servants whom he had made captive, and to take to himself all the

property saying, Our Lord Abram, Give me the persons, which you have rescued, and take the goods to yourself.

(Genesis 14:22) (Jasher 16:14...) (Jubilees 13:29...)
And Abram said to the kings of Sodom, As the Lord lives I have lifted up my hand to the Lord, the Most High God, the Possessor of heaven and earth, who redeemed my soul from all affliction, and who delivered me this day from my enemies, and gave them into my hand.

(Genesis 14:23) (...Jasher 16:14) (...Jubilees 13:29...)
That I will not take from a thread even to a shoe latchet, and that I will not take anything that is yours, lest you should say, I have made Abram rich: that you may not boast tomorrow, saying, Abram became rich from our property that he saved.

(Jasher 16:15)
For the Lord my God in whom I trust said to me, You shall lack nothing, for I will bless you in all the works of your hands.

(Genesis 14:24) (Jasher 16:16) (...Jubilees 13:29)
And now therefore behold, here is all belonging to you, take it and go; as the Lord lives I will not take from you from a living soul down to a shoe tie or thread, Save only the expense of the food that the young men who went out with me to battle have eaten, and the portion of the men which went with me, Aner, Eshcol, and Mamre, they and their men, as well as those also who had remained to watch the baggage, let them take their portion of the spoil.

(Jasher 16:17)
And the kings of Sodom gave Abram according to all that he had said, and they pressed him to take of whatever he chose, but he would not.

(Jasher 16:18)
And he sent away the kings of Sodom and the remainder of their men, and he gave them orders about Lot, and they went to their respective places.

(Jasher 16:19)
And Lot, his brother's son, he also sent away with his property, and he went with them, and Lot returned to his home, to Sodom, and Abram and his people returned to their home to the plains of Mamre, which is in Hebron.

Genesis: Chapter Fifteen

(Genesis 15:1) (Jasher 16:20...) (Jubilees 14:1)

At that time, after these things, in the fourth year of this week, on the new moon of the third month, the word of the Lord came to Abram in Hebron, in a vision, saying, Fear not, Abram: I am your shield, your defender, and your exceeding great reward.

(Genesis 15:2) (Jubilees 14:2...)

And Abram said, Lord God, what will you give me, seeing I go childless, and the son of Maseq, the son of my handmaid, the steward of my house is this Eliezer of Damascus? He will be my heir.

(Genesis 15:3) (...Jubilees 14:2)

And Abram said, Behold, You have given no seed to me: and, lo, one born in my house is my heir.

(Genesis 15:4) (Jubilees 14:3)

And, behold, the word of the Lord came to him, saying, This shall not be your heir; but he that shall come forth out of your own bowels shall be your heir.

(...Jasher 16:20)

For I will not leave you, until I shall have multiplied you, and blessed you and made your seed like the stars in heaven, which cannot be measured nor numbered.

(Genesis 15:5) (Jubilees 14:4, 5)

And He brought him forth abroad, and said, Look now toward

heaven, and tell the stars, if you are able to number them: And he looked toward heaven, and beheld the stars. And He said to him, So shall your seed be.

(Genesis 15:6) (Jubilees 14:6)
And he believed in the Lord; and He counted it to him for righteousness.

(Genesis 15:7) (Jasher 16:21) (Jubilees 14:7)
And He said to him, I am the Lord that brought you out of Ur of the Chaldees, to give you and to your seed all this land of the Canaanites that you see with your eyes to inherit it forever; and I will be God to you and to your seed after you, only be strong and do not fear, walk before me and be perfect .

(Genesis 15:8) (Jubilees 14:8)
And he said, Lord God, whereby shall I know that I shall inherit it?

(Genesis 15:9) (Jubilees 14:9)
And He said to him, Take me a heifer of three years old, and a she goat of three years old, and a ram of three years old, and a turtledove, and a young pigeon.

(Genesis 15:10) (Jubilees 14:10, 11)
And he took to him all these in the middle of the month and he dwelt at the oak of Mamre, which is near Hebron. And he built there an altar, and sacrificed all these; and he poured their blood on the altar, and divided them in the midst, and laid each piece one against another: but the birds he not divide.

(Genesis 15:11) (Jubilees 14:12)
And when the birds came down on the carcasses, Abram

drove them away and did not suffer the birds to touch them.

(Genesis 15:12) (Jubilees 14:13...)
And it came to pass, when the sun was going down, that an ecstasy, a deep sleep fell on Abram; and, lo, a horror of great darkness fell on him.

(Genesis 15:13) (...Jubilees 14:13)
And He said to Abram, Know of a surety that your seed shall be a stranger in a land that is not theirs, and shall serve them; and they shall afflict them four hundred years;

(Genesis 15:14) (Jubilees 14:14)
And also, that nation, whom they shall serve, I will judge: and afterward shall they come out with great substance.

(Genesis 15:15) (Jubilees 14:15)
And you shall go to your fathers in peace; you shall be buried in a good old age.

(Genesis 15:16) (Jubilees 14:16)
But in the fourth generation they shall come here again: for the iniquity of the Amorites is not yet full.

(Genesis 15:17) (Jubilees 14:17)
And it came to pass, that, when the sun went down, and it was dark, he awoke from his sleep, and he arose, behold a smoking furnace, and a burning lamp that passed between those pieces.

(Genesis 15:18) (Jubilees 14:18...)
In the same day, the Lord made a covenant with Abram, saying, To your seed have I given this land, from the river of Egypt to the great river, the river Euphrates:

(Genesis 15:19) (...Jubilees 14:18...)
The Kenites, and the Kenizzites, and the Kadmonites,

(Genesis 15:20) (...Jubilees 14:18...)
And the Hittites, and the Perizzites, and the Rephaims, the Phakorites, and the Hivites,

(Genesis 15:21) (...Jubilees 14:18)
And the Amorites, and the Canaanites, and the Girgashites, and the Jebusites.

(Jubilees 14:19)
And the day passed, and Abram offered the pieces, and the birds, and their fruit offerings, and their drink offerings, and the fire devoured them.

(Jubilees 14:20)
And on that day, we made a covenant with Abram, according as we had covenanted with Noah in this month; and Abram renewed the festival and ordinance for himself forever.

(Jubilees 14:21)
And Abram rejoiced, and made all these things known to Sarai his wife; and he believed that he would have seed, but she did not bear.

(Jasher 16:22)
And in the seventy-eighth year of the life of Abram, in that year died Reu, the son of Peleg, and all the days of Reu were two hundred and thirty-nine years, and he died.

Genesis: Chapter Sixteen

(Genesis 16:1) (Jasher 16:23)

Now Sarai, the daughter of Haran, Abram's wife was still barren in those days; she bore him no children, either son or daughter: and she had an handmaid, an Egyptian, whose name was Hagar.

(Jasher 16:25)

For Hagar learned all the ways of Sarai as Sarai taught her, she was not in any way deficient in following her good ways.

(Genesis 16:2) (Jasher 16:24...,26) (Jubilees 14:22, 23...)

And when she saw that she bore no children, Sarai said to Abram, Behold now, the Lord has restrained me from bearing: Behold here is my handmaid Hagar, I pray, go in to Hagar, my Egyptian maid; it may be that she may bring forth upon my knees, that I may obtain children to you by her. And Abram hearkened to the voice of Sarai, his wife, and said to her, Do so.

(Genesis 16:3) (...Jasher 16:24, 27) (...Jubilees 14:23)

And Sarai Abram's wife took Hagar her maid whom Pharaoh had given her, the Egyptian, after Abram had dwelt ten years in the land of Canaan, and gave her to her husband Abram to be his wife. This was the eighty-fifth year of Abram's life.

(Genesis 16:4) (Jasher 16:28, 29) (Jubilees 14:24...)

And Abram hearkened to the voice of his wife Sarai, and he took his handmaid Hagar and he went in to Hagar, and she conceived: and when Hagar saw that she had conceived, she rejoiced greatly, and her mistress was despised in her eyes and she said within herself, This can only be that I am better before God than Sarai my mistress, for all the days that my mistress has been with my Lord, she did not conceive, but me the Lord has caused in so short a time to conceive by him.

(Jasher 16:30)
And when Sarai saw that Hagar had conceived by Abram, Sarai was jealous of her handmaid, and Sarai said within herself, This is surely nothing else but that she must be better than I am.

(Genesis 16:5...) (Jasher 16:31)
And Sarai said to Abram, My wrong be on you: for at the time when you prayed before the Lord for children, why did you not pray on my account, that the Lord should give me seed from you?

(...Genesis 16:5) (Jasher 16:32)
I have given my maid into your bosom; and when she saw that she had conceived, I was despised in her eyes: And when I speak to Hagar in your presence, she despises my words, because she has conceived, and you will say nothing to her; may the Lord judge between me and you for what you have done to me.

(Genesis 16:6) (Jasher 16:33)
But Abram said to Sarai, Behold, your maid is in your hand; do to her as it pleases you. And when Sarai dealt hardly with her, she fled from her face to the wilderness.

(Genesis 16:7) (Jasher 16:34...)
And the angel of the Lord found her in the place where she had fled, by a fountain of water, a well in the wilderness, by

the fountain in the way to Shur.

(Genesis 16:8)
And he said, Hagar, Sarai's maid, where did you come from? And where will you go? And she said, I flee from the face of my mistress Sarai.

(Genesis 16:9) (...Jasher 16:34...)
And the angel of the Lord said to her, Return to your mistress, and submit yourself under her hands.

(Genesis 16:10) (...Jasher 16:34...)
And the angel of the Lord said to her, Do not fear, I will multiply your seed exceedingly, that it shall not be numbered for multitude.

(Genesis 16:11) (...Jasher 16:34)
And the angel of the Lord said to her, Behold, you are with child, and shall bear a son, and shall call his name Ishmael; because the Lord has heard your affliction.

(Genesis 16:12)
And he will be a wild man; his hand will be against every man, and every man's hand against him; and he shall dwell in the presence of all his brethren.

(Genesis 16:13)
And she called the name of the Lord that spoke to her, God sees me: for she said, Have I also looked here after Him that sees me?

(Genesis 16:14) (Jasher 16:35)
And Hagar called the place of the well was called Beerlahairoi; behold, it is between Kadesh and the wilderness of Bered.

(Genesis 16:15) (Jasher 16:36...) (...Jubilees 14:24...)
And Hagar at that time returned to her master's house. And at the end of days, Hagar bore Abram a son: and Abram called his son's name, which Hagar bore, Ishmael, in the fifth year of this week.

(Genesis 16:16) (...Jasher 16:36) (...Jubilees 14:24)
And Abram was eighty-six years old, when Hagar bore Ishmael to Abram.

(Jasher 17:1)
And in those days, in the ninety-first year of the life of Abram, the children of Chittim made war with the children of Tubal, for when the Lord had scattered the sons of men upon the face of the earth, the children of Chittim went and embodied themselves in the plain of Canopia, and they built themselves cities there and dwelt by the river Tibreu.

(Jasher 17:2)
And the children of Tubal dwelt in Tuscanah, and their boundaries reached the river Tibreu, and the children of Tubal built a city in Tuscanan, and they called the name Sabinah, after the name of Sabinah son of Tubal their father, and they dwelt there to this day.

(Jasher 17:3)
And it was at that time the children of Chittim made war with the children of Tubal, and the children of Tubal were smitten before the children of Chittim, and the children of Chittim caused three hundred and seventy men to fall from the children of Tubal.

(Jasher 17:4)
And at that time the children of Tubal swore to the children

of Chittim, saying, You shall not intermarry among us, and no man shall give his daughter to any of the sons of Chittim.

(Jasher 17:5)
For all the daughters of Tubal were in those days fair, for no women were then found in the whole earth so fair as the daughters of Tubal.

(Jasher 17:6)
And all who delighted in the beauty of women went to the daughters of Tubal and took wives from them, and the sons of men, kings and princes, who greatly delighted in the beauty of women, took wives in those days from the daughters of Tubal.

(Jasher 17:7)
And at the end of three years after the children of Tubal had sworn to the children of Chittim not to give them their daughters for wives, about twenty men of the children of Chittim went to take some of the daughters of Tubal, but they found none.

(Jasher 17:8)
For the children of Tubal kept their oaths not to intermarry with them, and they would not break their oaths.

(Jasher 17:9)
And in the days of harvest the children of Tubal went into their fields to get in their harvest, when the young men of Chittim assembled and went to the city of Sabinah, and each man took a young woman from the daughters of Tubal, and they came to their cities.

(Jasher 17:10)
And the children of Tubal heard of it and they went to make

war with them, and they could not prevail over them, for the mountain was exceedingly high from them, and when they saw they could not prevail over them they returned to their land.

(Jasher 17:11)
And at the revolution of the year the children of Tubal went and hired about ten thousand men from those cities that were near them, and they went to war with the children of Chittim.

(Jasher 17:12)
And the children of Tubal went to war with the children of Chittim, to destroy their land and to distress them, and in this engagement the children of Tubal prevailed over the children of Chittim, and the children of Chittim, seeing that they were greatly distressed, lifted up the children which they had by the daughters of Tubal, upon the wall which had been built, to be before the eyes of the children of Tubal.

(Jasher 17:13)
And the children of Chittim said to them, Have you come to make war with your own sons and daughters, and have we not been considered your flesh and bones from that time till now?

(Jasher 17:14)
And when the children of Tubal heard this they ceased to make war with the children of Chittim, and they went away.

(Jasher 17:15)
And they returned to their cities, and the children of Chittim at that time assembled and built two cities by the sea, and they called one Purtu and the other Ariza.

Genesis: Chapter Seventeen

(Jubilees 15:1)
And in the fifth year of the fourth week of this jubilee, in the third month, in the middle of the month, Abram celebrated the feast of the first-fruits of the grain harvest.

(Jubilees 15:2)
And he offered new offerings on the altar, the first fruits of the produce, to the Lord, a heifer and a goat and a sheep on the altar as a burnt sacrifice to the Lord; their fruit offerings and their drink offerings he offered on the altar with frankincense.

(Genesis 17:1) (Jasher 17:16, 17...) (Jubilees 15:3)
And when Abram was ninety-nine years old, the Lord appeared to Abram, and said to him, I am the Almighty God; walk before Me, approve yourself before me, and be perfect.

(Genesis 17:2) (...Jasher 17:17...) (Jubilees 15:4)
And I will make My covenant between Me and you, and I will multiply your seed exceedingly.

(Genesis 17:3) (Jubilees 15:5)
And Abram fell on his face: and God talked with Him, saying,

(Genesis 17:4) (...Jasher 17:20) (Jubilees 15:6)
As for Me, behold, My covenant is with you, and you shall be a father of many nations.

(Genesis 17:5) (Jasher 17:19...) (Jubilees 15:7)
Neither shall your name any more be called Abram, but your

name shall be Abraham from here after, even forever; for I have made you a father of many nations.

(Genesis 17:6) (Jubilees 15:8)
And I will make you exceeding fruitful, and I will make nations of you, and kings shall come out of you.

(Genesis 17:7) (Jubilees 15:9)
And I will establish My covenant between Me and you and your seed after you in their generations for an everlasting covenant, to be a God to you, and to your seed after you.

(Genesis 17:8) (Jubilees 15:10)
And I will give to you, and to your seed after you, the land wherein you are a stranger, all the land of Canaan, for an everlasting possession; and I will be their God.

(Genesis 17:9) (Jubilees 15:11...)
And the Lord God said to Abraham, And as for you, you shall keep My covenant therefore, you, and your seed after you in their generations.

(Genesis 17:10) (...Jasher 17:17) (...Jubilees 15:11...)
This is My covenant, which you shall keep, which I make between Me and you and your seed after you; Every man child among you shall be circumcised.

(Genesis 17:11) (...Jubilees 15:11)
And you shall circumcise the flesh of your foreskin; and it shall be a token of the covenant between Me and you.

(Genesis 17:12) (Jasher 17:18...) (Jubilees 15:12)
And he that is eight days old shall be circumcised among you, every man child in your generations, he that is born in the

house, or bought with money of any stranger, whom you have acquired which is not of your seed.

(Genesis 17:13) (...Jasher 17:18) (Jubilees 15:13)
He that is born in your house, and he that is bought with your money, must needs be circumcised, and those whom you have bought with money shall be circumcised: and My covenant shall be in your flesh for an everlasting covenant.

(Genesis 17:14) (Jubilees 15:14)
And the uncircumcised man child whose flesh of his foreskin is not circumcised on the eighth day, that soul shall be cut off from his people; he has broken My covenant.

(Genesis 17:15) (...Jasher 17:19) (Jubilees 15:15)
And God said to Abraham, As for Sarai your wife, you shall not call her name Sarai, but her name shall be Sarah.

(Genesis 17:16) (...Jasher 17:20) (Jubilees 15:16)
And I will bless her, and give you a son also of her: and I will multiply your seed after you yea, I will bless her, and she shall be a mother of nations; and I will bless him, and he shall become a nation; kings of people shall be of her. And kings of nations shall proceed from him.

(Genesis 17:17) (Jubilees 15:17)
Then Abraham fell on his face, and laughed and rejoiced, and said in his heart, Shall a child be born to him that is a hundred years old? And shall Sarah, that is ninety years old, bear?

(Genesis 17:18) (Jubilees 15:18)
And Abraham said to God, O that Ishmael might live before you!

(Genesis 17:19) (Jubilees 15:19)
And God said, Yea, and Sarah your wife shall also bear you a son indeed; and you shall call his name Isaac: and I will establish My covenant with him for an everlasting covenant, and with his seed after him.

(Genesis 17:20) (Jubilees 15:20)
And as for Ishmael, I have also heard you: Behold, I have blessed him, and will make him fruitful, and make him great, and will multiply him exceedingly; twelve princes shall he beget, and I will make him a great nation.

(Genesis 17:21) (Jubilees 15:21)
But My covenant will I establish with Isaac, which Sarah shall bear to you at this set time in the next year.

(Genesis 17:22) (Jubilees 15:22)
And he left off talking with him, and God went up from Abraham.

(Genesis 17:23) (Jasher 18:1) (Jubilees 15:23)
And Abraham rose and did all that God had ordered him. And Abraham took Ishmael his son, the men of his household and all that were born in his house, and all that were bought with his money, every male among the men of Abraham's house; and circumcised the flesh of their foreskin in the selfsame day, as God had said to him.

(Jasher 18:2...)
And there was not one left whom he did not circumcise, and Abraham and his son Ishmael were circumcised in the flesh of their foreskin;

(Genesis 17:24)

And Abraham was ninety years old and nine, when he was circumcised in the flesh of his foreskin.

(Genesis 17:25) (Jasher 18:2)

And Ishmael his son was thirteen years old, when he was circumcised in the flesh of his foreskin.

(Genesis 17:26) (Jubilees 15:24...)

In the selfsame day was Abraham circumcised, and Ishmael his son.

(Genesis 17:27) (...Jubilees 15:24)

And all the men of his house, born in the house, and bought with money of the stranger, were circumcised with him.

Epilogue

(Jubilees 15:25)
This law is for all the generations forever, and there is no circumcision of the days, and no omission of one day out of the eight days; for it is an eternal ordinance, ordained and written on the heavenly tablets.

(Jubilees 15:26)
And everyone that is born, the flesh of whose foreskin is not circumcised on the eighth day, belongs not to the children of the covenant which the Lord made with Abraham, but to the children of destruction; nor is there, moreover, any sign on him that he is the Lord's, but he is destined to be destroyed and slain from the earth, and to be rooted out of the earth, for he has broken the covenant of the Lord our God.

(Jubilees 15:27)
For all the angels of the presence and all the angels of sanctification have been so created from the day of their creation, and before the angels of the presence and the angels of sanctification He has sanctified Israel, that they should be with Him and with His holy angels.

(Jubilees 15:28)
And do you command the children of Israel and let them observe the sign of this covenant for their generations as an eternal ordinance, and they will not be rooted out of the land.

(Jubilees 15:29)
For the command is ordained for a covenant, that they should observe it forever among all the children of Israel.

(Jubilees 15:30)
For Ishmael and his sons and his brothers and Esau, the Lord did not cause to approach Him, and he chose them not because they are the children of Abraham, because He knew them, but He chose Israel to be His people.

(Jubilees 15:31)
And He sanctified it, and gathered it from among all the children of men; for there are many nations and many peoples, and all are His, and over all has He placed spirits in authority to lead them astray from Him.

(Jubilees 15:32)
But over Israel He did not appoint any angel or spirit, for He alone is their ruler, and He will preserve them and require them at the hand of His angels and His spirits, and at the hand of all His powers in order that He may preserve them and bless them, and that they may be His and He may be theirs from here after, forever.

(Jubilees 15:33)
And now I announce to you that the children of Israel will not keep true to this ordinance, and they will not circumcise their sons according to all this law; for in the flesh of their circumcision they will omit this circumcision of their sons, and all of them, sons of Beliar, will leave their sons uncircumcised as they were born.

(Jubilees 15:34)
And there will be great wrath from the Lord against the children of Israel. Because they have forsaken His covenant and turned aside from His word, and provoked and blasphemed, inasmuch as they do not observe the ordinance of this law; for they have treated their members like the Gentiles, so that

they may be removed and rooted out of the land. And there will no more be pardon or forgiveness to them so that there should be forgiveness and pardon for all the sin of this eternal error.

Final Notes

We hope your journey is enriched and you are blessed through the production of the **Ancient Texts and the Bible** series!

Minister 2 Others would like to hear from you. If you have comments or questions concerning our materials, or if you find errors in our projects, misspellings, or formatting issues. We work hard to provide quality materials, however, sometimes things can squeak by unnoticed. Your feedback is truly appreciated.

We love producing helpful, innovative books and we are grateful for your support! If you have enjoyed this production, please consider writing a review and letting others know about our materials.

If you would like to be updated when we release new books and other materials, please sign up for our e-newsletter on our website.

Thanks!

Minister 2 Others

Minister2others.com

www.ingramcontent.com/pod-product-compliance
Lightning Source LLC
Chambersburg PA
CBHW071255190726
48292CB00007B/2545

* 9 7 8 1 9 4 7 7 5 1 2 0 0 *